High-Poverty, High-Performing Schools

Foundations for

A division of
ROWMAN & LITTLEFIELD PUBLISHERS, INC.
Lanham • New York • Toronto • Plymouth, UK

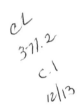

Published by Rowman & Littlefield Education
A division of Rowman & Littlefield Publishers, Inc.
A wholly owned subsidiary of The Rowman & Littlefield Publishing Group, Inc.
4501 Forbes Boulevard, Suite 200, Lanham, Maryland 20706
http://www.rowmaneducation.com
Estover Road, Plymouth PL6 7PY, United Kingdom

British Library Cataloguing in Publication Information Available

Library of Congress Cataloging-in-Publication Data
Wong, Ovid K.
  High-poverty, high-performing schools : foundations for real student success / Ovid K. Wong.
      p. cm.
  Includes bibliographical references and index.
  ISBN 978-1-60709-789-1 (cloth : alk. paper) — ISBN 978-1-60709-790-7 (pbk. : alk. paper) — ISBN 978-1-60709-791-4 (electronic : alk. paper)
  1. Poor children—Education—United States. 2. Children with social disabilities—Education—United States. 3. School improvement programs—United States. 4. Academic achievement—United States. I. Title.
  LC4091.W655 2012
  371.2'07—dc23   2011027935

∞™ The paper used in this publication meets the minimum requirements of American National Standard for Information Sciences—Permanence of Paper for Printed Library Materials, ANSI/NISO Z39.48-1992.

Printed in the United States of America

Contents

Figures

Foreword

Poverty and its attendant effects on education outcomes is an issue that won't disappear. For some, poverty is chronic; for others, generational; and for some others, temporary. But for all, poverty grinds down hopes, aspirations, and performance with few exceptions. These words come as no surprise to anyone. The question for educators is how to confront a culture of school failure, turn it around, and give hope to the children of poverty. As a nation, we cannot allow so much of our brainpower to go unrealized. Our nation needs strong contributions from all its citizens if we are to remain a leader in the global economy.

In schools, children from high-poverty environments, as a group, underperform their more affluent classmates. Said differently, study after study has shown that children of high socioeconomic levels outperform their classmates of lesser means. However, the problem is not intractable. There are islands of hope among our many schools. Some of these successful schools are bridging the poverty gap and producing high-performing students even when all the statistics suggest they should not succeed. How are these few schools able to raise the educational performance level of their impoverished students when so many schools and teachers have failed for so long? The question is not rhetorical. There are answers—answers that can be duplicated in all settings. These answers are for all to see in the education research literature and through the close examination of schools that have succeeded in showing dramatic improvement in pupil performance. The effective schools, identified as high-poverty, high-performing schools, are ones that actually practice what they preach. They are schools that implement good management and classroom practices in a systematic, enthusiastic, and sustainable way.

In this book, Professor Wong provides a comprehensive and detailed examination of several schools with documented success in raising the performance of students from high-poverty environments. These several schools have a sufficient number of common attributes to enable Professor Wong to create a model of success independent of charismatic individuals. Professor Wong also includes from education research literature descriptions of the training, knowledge, and skills necessary to effectively overcome the high-poverty, low-performance culture.

The high-poverty, high-performing, or 2(HP), schools described in this book are found in seven states ranging from the West Coast to the East Coast and from North to South. The 2(HP) schools were identified as such through the use of student and school demographics and student performance.

When one examines the characteristics of the 2(HP) schools, the most pervasive attribute is one of shared high expectations for all, by all. "High expectations for all" means that high performance is expected of administrators, teachers, and community, not just students. For such an environment to be realized, there must be a strong commitment from all stakeholders with the expectation that administrators, teachers, students, and the community will all work toward reform implementation. Reform requires a clear and shared vision of what is to be accomplished and the ability to mobilize all necessary resources, both human and material.

Another common attribute of 2(HP) schools is a well-defined school program carefully aligned with state guidelines. Alignment, however, is not enough. There must also be a data trail. Student performance in 2(HP) schools is measured frequently relative to expectations. Performance reports are created by teachers and counselors for school administrators and parents. Students at risk are quickly identified and the appropriate interventions are made. Learning problems are kept manageable and not allowed to balloon into major learning roadblocks. Students are encouraged and provided with the help needed to maintain a positive self-image. For those students for whom English is a second language, instruction is provided in the student's native language, if possible, until the student becomes proficient enough in English to show measurable benefits.

Community involvement is high in 2(HP) schools. High-poverty, high-performing school communities accept and support changes required to improve the performance of high-poverty students. Contributions of money and materials, while welcome, are not enough. Parents of students in 2(HP) schools spend time in the classroom through volunteer activities and continue to support the school program at home after the school day.

When one examines 2(HP) schools, one finds a cadre of strong teachers. Strong teachers have expectations as high for themselves as for the students. These are teachers who know the principles of good teaching, who practice good teaching, and who are willing to work toward the collective goal of success for all students. Effective teachers use a variety of good practices individually and in collaboration with others to meet expectations. They work hard. They set high expectations for their students and do what is necessary to provide an environment for success.

What are these good practices? How does one recognize them? Where can they be found? In truth, good practice has been around in one form or another since the time of Socrates. Effective teachers have used various forms of effective practice from generation to generation depending on their expectations for student performance. However, schools that wish to reform their practices already have a teaching staff in place. What resources exist for those teachers who wish to become more effective? As the reader will find, resources are many, but as with any change, there must be strong leadership from administrators, a clear vision of the change required, obtainable goals, and support provided in terms of time and resources. Finally, teachers must agree that they too want change and are willing to give up old practices and develop more effective teaching skills. Teachers unwilling to change may have to be reassigned.

Undeniably, strong leadership is the key to any successful change model. Overcoming the culture of failure attendant with high-poverty students/high-poverty schools calls for a yeomanlike effort on the part of all school administrators, but in particular the school principal. Even with a clear vision for reform and a willing staff, the principal must possess the skills and knowledge necessary to initiate change and to sustain it over the long term. The culture of failure is strongly entrenched in many students, schools, and communities and was not easy to change in 2(HP) schools described in this book. Consider how difficult it is to raise expectations for school performance when few in a high-poverty community have been successful in school.

The principal, by job description, is required to lead a staff of professionals in implementing and administering the school program and to make sure that teachers maintain their skills and knowledge. To realize success, the principal in 2(HP) schools is an effective communicator with teachers, staff, parents, and the community. Through the teachers and staff, the principal is able to assess student needs and to respond accordingly while at the same time making sure that local, state, and federal requirements are met. The principal is a supervisor of teachers, providing support when the program is implemented according to plan and redirecting in a positive way when it is not. The list could go on in much greater detail, as the reader will learn in the body of the text. In the case of schools with a large number of high-poverty students, the principal's role becomes even more acute given the need to change so much in terms of the whole school culture where failure has been the norm and where past efforts to improve student performance have failed. Working with people is not easy. Working to bring success to a school program with people accustomed to failure is even harder.

So far nothing has been said about what should be taught in the classroom. How do the principal, the teachers, the community, the state, the professional associations, and others who might have a say in the school program decide what needs to be taught to bring about more of these successful 2(HP) schools? To say the least, there are many sources for input. In fact, there are so many that the task of choosing is daunting, if not overwhelming.

The textbook remains the teacher's primary source of information. Many textbooks are part of a carefully developed series produced by a number of different publishing companies. Textbook content is usually written by or under the guidance of a professional team in the field, such as mathematics or science. The textbook often answers the teacher's need for what to teach and in what order. As professional educators, teachers must decide if the textbook under consideration meets the needs of the all the children, most of the children, or only some of the children. As in so many cases, and especially education, one size does not fit all. As will be illustrated by Professor Wong, no matter how many children there are in the classroom, each one will learn in many different ways, and therefore, will need to obtain information from many sources for use in many different learning environments. A single teaching/learning source has never been and will never be sufficient for effective learning for all. When trying to overcome a culture of failure, 2(HP) schools use textbooks as only one of many teaching/learning resources. In the final consideration of a textbook, the teacher will have to assess what parts of the text conform to explicit guidelines and standards for that subject, at that grade level, at that school, in that school district, and in that state. In 2(HP) schools, textbooks become one of many resources for developing a curriculum, but not the only one.

For a number of years now, public education across the nation has been moving toward a standards-based curriculum with attendant statewide testing to determine if schools are meeting the standards. In the case of 2(HP) schools, state standards become the curriculum foundation. All 2(HP) schools follow their respective state standards without exception; this makes sense only if school success is going to be measured by state-developed tests designed to measure student performance relative to the standards. Performance on state-mandated tests has become the measure of student, teacher, and school success for 2(HP) schools.

Standards are what thoughtful educators consider to be the necessary set of knowledge and skills to become an effective citizen in a democratic society. However, neither all students nor all schools meet the standards in the same way. With support from the principal and the professional knowledge of strong teachers, 2(HP) schools find ways for students from many backgrounds, with different learning needs, and different preferred ways of learning to meet established standards. The reader will recognize these standards for what they are independent of having been developed at the local, state, or federal level.

Professional organizations and societies represent another source of standards. Standards established by professional organizations do not have to be met by schools. Nonetheless, they serve a very important role in that they have become the primary resource for those writing state standards specific to each subject area measured by the state. In that respect, standards established by such groups as the National Science Teachers Association and the National Council of Mathematics Teachers, to name but two, have been indispensable.

As one might expect, standards have little effect and could easily be ignored if not measured. Statewide tests given at different grade levels as determined by the state provide the vehicle for measuring student and school success. In 2(HP) schools, teachers and administrators do not wait for state tests to be administered to assess the progress of their students. Testing, both formal and informal, goes on all the time in 2(HP) schools. To wait for the results of state tests every few years is to wait too long for information needed to help children at risk. Teachers need to know on a regular basis how their children are performing, hence the frequent assessment practices found in 2(HP) schools.

Finally, chapter 7, which describes the 2(HP) model, has been very carefully crafted by Professor Wong and should be read more than once. In truth, the model needs to be systemic if there is to be change in how one plots a road to success with students and schools that have failed for so long; but for which success is not only possible but expected. Schools and teachers cannot be considered successful if only a few students succeed. Likewise, we cannot consider our nationwide education system to be successful if a significant portion of students fail. Professor Wong's description of 2(HP) schools is a model of good education at any level for any school. Whether a beginning teacher or veteran educator, every reader will benefit from the inspiring success stories and reliable teaching pathways found within these pages. Good management and good classroom practice benefit all students, not just low-performing ones.

John P. Smith
Associate Professor Emeritus
University of Washington, Seattle

Introduction

People interested in finding a nice place to live, raise a family, or retire often look to quality local schools as a major decision factor. To many, school is a reflection of school community quality for the simple fact that an average of 70% of the local tax dollars go to support local schools. Tax dollars buy resources, and resources support schools. Using this simple money-stream formula one would reasonably expect to find successful schools in a low-poverty community.

The social reproduction theory seems to support one classification of schools based on community resources and student success. The two opposite ends of the classification are the low-poverty (or rich), high-performing schools and the high-poverty (or poor), low-performing schools. If the social reproduction theory is used to predict school success, then the likely place to find high-performing schools will be the wealthy communities. Why? Because money, power, and student success work together closely in school operations (Wong and Casing 2010).

While low-performing schools in a low-poverty community are generally common, this should not be taken as the absolute. There are exceptions to the rule. There are schools with high-performing students in the midst of impoverished communities. In the wake of the school reform movement, it is important to understand the foundation of real school success connecting to effective school leadership, curriculum, instruction, and assessment regardless of the community's social economic status.

Welcome to the quest for the high-poverty, high-performing schools—the holy grail of student and school success!

REFERENCE

Wong, O., and D. Casing. 2010. *Equalize student achievement: Prioritize money and power.* Lanham, MD: Rowman & Littlefield Education.

Chapter One

In Search of Excellent Schools

1.1. WHAT IS THE STATE OF EDUCATION IN THE UNITED STATES?

The United States conducts an official count of its population every 10 years. In census 2010, the count provides basic information about race, gender, age, number in the household, and contact information with 10 questions. How does the nation keep current about its population if the census is done only once every 10 years? Fortunately, there are other more frequent but smaller sample surveys. In addition to the decennial census, the American Community Survey (ACS) collects supplemental demographic, housing, and socioeconomic information to include education status of the population every year. The responsibility of the supplemental survey has fallen to the U.S. Census Bureau since 1942.

Do you know that the census came from the Constitution of the United States of America? Figure 1.1 describes the brief history of the U.S. census. In 1787, the United States became the first nation to make census mandatory in its constitution. In 1790, the people-counting process started primarily for taxation and military drafting purposes. The labor-intensive process took a total of 18 months. In 1792, the first census results were submitted to President Washington. Every 10 years after the very first one, a census has been conducted.

Over the years, the census changed and evolved many times over. In 1810, Congress decided that while the population needed to be counted, other important information was needed to make informed decisions and fund appropriations. Thus, the first census in the field of manufacturing began. Later, censuses on agriculture, construction, mining, housing, local governments, commerce, transportation, and business were included. In 1840, education as a survey category was first included in the U.S. census questionnaire. The purpose of the questionnaire is to find information about the status of education of its populace.

Let us fast-forward 152 years. In 1992, data on educational attainment were derived from a single census question asking the highest grade level of school completed, or the highest degree received. The single educational attainment question now in use

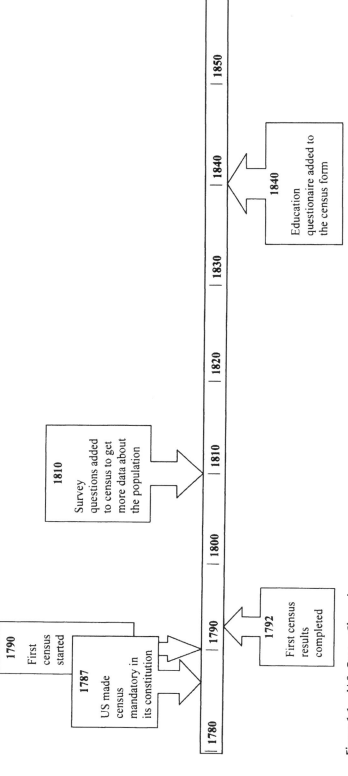

Figure 1.1. U.S. Census Chronology
Source: U.S. Census Bureau. www.census.gov/history/www/through_the_decades/overview/

was introduced in the Current Population Survey beginning January 1992, and it is similar to that used in the 1990 Decennial Census of Population and Housing.

In June 2004, the U.S. Census Bureau published a report about the educational attainment in the United States. Among the many items asked in the census form, there was a question regarding the highest grade or degree completed. The answer to the question was used to determine the educational attainment of the population. The information is also used to assess the socioeconomic conditions of school-age children. Government agencies carefully analyze the data for funding allocations and program planning and implementation.

Furthermore, in order to meet statutory requirement under the Voting Rights Act, the data are needed to determine the literacy status of citizens in language minority groups. The act outlaws the practice of requiring otherwise qualified voters to pass literacy tests in order to register to vote.

The 2004 report finds that the population in the United States is becoming more educated. Specifically, the educational attainment of young adults (25 to 29 years of age), who represent the future of the country, shows dramatic improvement by groups who have historically been less educated. Nevertheless, significant differences remain across the 50 states. The percentage of high school graduate or more ranges from 91% in New Hampshire to 77.5% in Texas, with the national average at 85.9% (Educational Attainment in the United States: 2003; U.S. Census Bureau 2004). Two questions similar to the 2004 survey are found in the 2010 census. The questions represent school-level enrollment and school achievement.

One interesting aspect of the census report is the statistics presentation with no cause interpretation. For that reason, many researchers dig deep into the census data and render their expertise to find meaning behind the information.

Two hypotheses related to the social and economic factors are proposed in an attempt to study what accounts for the different levels of educational attainment. Is the level of educational attainment related to the level of poverty? Specifically, is the level of educational attainment related to the level of household income? Figure 1.2 is a list presenting a sample of 18 states in 2000 with reference to the percentage of poverty level, the percentage of median household income, and the percentage of high school graduate or more (to represent educational achievement).

The connections between educational achievement and poverty represented by income in figure 1.2 are not surprising. There is a significant negative correlation between poverty and educational achievement (correlation = -0.871). These statistics data mean that, in general, the high level of poverty correlates to the low level of educational attainment. There is another specific correlation between poverty and median household income (correlation = -0.899). This means that, in general, the high level of poverty correlates to the low median household income. If the level of household income is controlled statistically (i.e., partial correlation), the correlation between poverty and educational attainment drops from -0.899 to -0.796. Still, the statistics seem to support the common belief that students perform poorly in poor schools and vice versa.

1.2. WHAT ARE THE BLUE RIBBON SCHOOLS?

The Blue Ribbon award is given to schools that achieve the top 10% of their state's testing scores for several years, or show significant student achievement gains. The

State	1999 median household income	1999 % below poverty level	2000 % H.S. graduate or more
Alaska	$51,571	9	88.3
Arizona	$40,412	13.9	81
California	$47,493	12.5	76.8
Connecticut	$53,935	7.9	84
Delaware	$47,381	8.7	82.6
Georgia	$42,433	13	78.6
Hawaii	$49,820	8.3	84.6
Illinois	$46,590	11.9	81.4
Louisiana	$32,566	19.6	74.8
Maryland	$52,868	8.3	83.8
Mississippi	$31,330	19.9	72.9
Nebraska	$39,250	9.7	86.6
New Hanpshire	$49,467	6.5	87.4
New Jersey	$55,146	8.5	82.1
New Mexico	$34,133	18.4	78.9
Oklahoma	$33,400	14.7	80.6
Texas	$39,927	15.4	75.7
West Virginia	$29,696	17.9	75.2

Figure 1.2.   Selected States by Social Economic Status and High School Completion
Source: U.S. Census Bureau, 1999.

Blue Ribbon is considered the highest honor a school can achieve. The award was established in 1982 by Secretary of Education Terrell Bell.

The program initially honored only secondary schools. It was expanded to include primary schools. It was later changed again to honor secondary schools and primary schools in alternate years. The Blue Ribbon program cites about 4% of schools per year out of 133,000 public, charter, private, and parochial schools. What makes a Blue Ribbon school?

To be selected for the Blue Ribbon recognition, a school must have been in existence for five years. It has to conduct a self-assessment of strengths and weaknesses with plans for improvement. The school turns in a paper application that includes information about its progress toward reaching the National Education Goals. The application is then reviewed by a panel of experts to select the most promising schools for site visits. The panel evaluates the reports and finally makes recommendations to the U.S. secretary of education to announce the winning schools.

An analysis of the Blue Ribbon schools reveals the fact that students who come from homes with higher income and better-educated parents did better academically by virtue of their social economic background. One year, eight schools in Pennsylvania received the award. Seven out of the eight schools had above-state-average household income; two of the schools were in the wealthiest community in the state. In another year, 13 Illinois public schools received the award; all of them were in the above-the-state-average-income category. A good way to generalize the traits of the prestigious Blue Ribbon award schools is that they are wealthy and high achieving.

1.3. WHAT IS *BUSINESS WEEK'S* CHOICE OF SCHOOL COMMUNITIES?

Finding a nice community to live, raise families, or retire in has always been a challenge for many people. The challenge comes from the fact that there are many factors that go into the search. The factors may include safety, price of housing, recreation facilities, school quality, transportation, hospitals, and other community services. More important, the person making the community selection needs to carefully prioritize the factors to determine what he considers to be the best.

For several years *Business Week* has been annually analyzing towns in America and ranking the best places to raise families. The criteria used in the analysis are school performance, number of schools, household expenditures, crime rates, air quality, job growth, family income, museums, parks, theaters, other amenities, and diversity. Affordability, safety, and school test scores are given the heaviest weight in the ranking. The 2010 overall top winner is Tinley Park. Where is Tinley Park, and what is the community like?

Tinley Park is a suburban community in Illinois. It is 25 miles southwest of metropolitan Chicago. The population was 58,322 in the 2007 census. It is one of the fastest-growing suburbs of Chicago. Named after the village's first railroad master in the 1800s, Tinley Park has two train stations, which carry commuters to downtown Chicago. Young families are moving to Tinley Park for the same reason that old-timers chose to raise their children there 35 years ago. They look at the schools, the community services, and a home that is also good for the pocketbook. For growing families, school quality is on top of the priority list. Let us find out more about the Tinley Park schools.

The Tinley Park community is served by five school districts. These school districts are Arbor Park School District 145, Bremen Community High School District 228, Kirby School District 140, Summit Hill School District 161, and Tinley Park Consolidated School District 146. In 2009, the five school districts and their average percentage of low-income students was approximately 17%. Low-income students are students qualifying for free and reduced school lunch. How did the low-income student percentages in Tinley Park compare to the rest of the Illinois public schools? The 2009 Illinois average of low-income students was 42.9%. In other words, Tinley Park schools were below the state average in low-income students, and the schools had comparatively more and better school resources. More important to the resources of the community is the academic performance of the students. Let us look at that next.

School District	% Low Income	Meet Reading AYP	Meet Math AYP
Arbor Park	28.6%	No	No
Bremen	25.8%	No	No
Kirby	2.3%	Yes	Yes
Summit Hill	4.7%	Yes	Yes
Tinley Park	23.3%	No	Yes

Figure 1.3.   Tinley Park Schools AYP
Source: Printed with permission from the Illinois State Board of Education.

Under the No Child Left Behind (NCLB) law, students at designated grade level shall meet and exceed a predetermined reading and mathematics performance level every year. This predetermined level of performance is called the Adequate Yearly Progress (AYP). How was student performance in Tinley Park measured against the Illinois AYP in 2009? Figure 1.3 shows that the 2009 state report card on public schools in Tinley Park had mixed results.

Correlating the percentage of low-income students to student performance, one can generalize that low poverty tends to favor high student performance. Critics argue that Tinley Park may not be a large enough sample to support the generalization. Interestingly, even if the scope of the sample widens, the same generalization still prevails study after study. Is this not what we just discussed in the previous sections? Check out the top-performing schools in your area, region, or state. Find the connection between poverty level and student performance. Are you now convinced that it is more likely that there will be good schools in low-poverty communities?

1.4. DOES POVERTY REALLY MATTER IN EDUCATION?

Historically, the adverse effects of poverty on student performance are well documented. In general, schools with high concentrations of low-income students have lower achievement test scores than schools with low concentrations of low-income students. A landmark study of the relationship between socioeconomic characteristics and student performance was reported in the mid-1960s.

Life in the 1960s took a turn from the relative calm of the 1950s. The children of the baby boom came of age. The civil rights movement and the Vietnam War put the nation into turmoil. A noisy minority of the baby boomers protested through demonstrations and attempted to change the direction of society. The brief time line provides insight into the turbulent decade of war, war protest, and hippies. In 1960, President Eisenhower signed the Civil Rights Acts into law.

In 1964, the Civil Rights law prompted an investigation concerning the disparity of educational opportunity by race, color, religion, or national origin in public schools. Following this law in 1966, James S. Coleman, then a professor at Johns Hopkins

University, was commissioned by Congress to study a very large sample of schools. The sample consisted of 600,000 children in 4,000 schools.

Coleman and his research team reported that most children attended schools where they were the majority race. While schooling between white and minority schools was similar, teachers' preparation, teachers' salaries, and curriculum were also similar. Despite the similarities, the results sadly found that minority children were a few years behind whites in school performance. The student achievement gap widened further by the high school years. In conclusion, the report pointed to the possible relationship between academic achievement and family background in the early years of schooling. Furthermore, going to segregated schools led to a greater academic disparity between whites and blacks.

The following year, another study conducted by the Civil Rights Commission, Racial Isolation in the Public Schools, confirmed Coleman's findings. Little did Coleman realize that his work later had a profound impact on government education policy. The government introduced a policy of affirmative action to integrate schools racially. The purpose of the affirmative policy was to end the de facto population segregation created by income level and ethnic neighborhood. A result of the policy was the busing of schoolchildren to schools outside their neighborhoods. The aim was to achieve a racial balance between schools by preventing disproportional minority student enrollment. For many years, the Coleman findings were held unchallenged. Nobody was able to redefine the important impact of resources on student achievement.

In 1997, Professor Thomas Guskey of the University of Kentucky published a report investigating the relationship between socioeconomic variables and school-level results. The study gathered student work portfolios, assessment test scores, and student performance in the areas of mathematics, science, social studies, arts and humanities, practical living, and vocational skills. The information was collected over a three-year period from 49 schools.

Guskey found that a single socioeconomic variable represented by the percentage of students qualifying for free or reduced school lunch explains a large portion of the variance in scores at all school levels. Correlations between the percentage of students in a school qualifying for free or reduced school lunch and the percentage of minority students are 0.82, 0.92, and 0.96 for elementary, middle, and high schools. In other words, the relationship between poverty and student achievement measures is greater at the high school level than at the elementary and middle school levels. The generalization of the Guskey study is limiting according to critics because the data collected are based on a single school district in Kentucky.

Based on the previous studies and according to the poverty and student performance variables, schools may be classified into four types. These schools are high-poverty, high-performing; high-poverty, low-performing; low-poverty, low-performing; and low-poverty, high-performing (figure 1.4).

The frequency distribution of the four school types in Illinois in 2001 is shown in figure 1.5. The most frequent school type is low poverty and high performing (79%), and 68% of those schools are in cities outside Chicago. The majority of the high-poverty, low-performing schools (62%) are in Chicago. The majority (47%) of high-poverty, high-performing schools are in the rural communities. Last, there are no low-poverty, low-performing schools because wealthy but low-performing schools are nonexistent in this study and they may be only a theoretical school type.

Low Performing   High Performing

	Low Performing	High Performing
High Poverty	High poverty low performing	High poverty high performing
Low Poverty	Low poverty low performing	Low poverty high performing

Figure 1.4.   School Types by Poverty and Performance
Source: Courtesy of the author.

In short, as concerns the state of education, the U.S. census, the profile of the Blue Ribbon schools, the analysis of *Business Week*'s choice of school communities, the research by Coleman and Guskey, and the 2001 frequency distribution of Illinois school types all point to the critical impact of a community's social economic status on student success. Based on this generalization, one would expect to find high academic success more in a wealthy environment than in an impoverished environment. One would also expect to find successful schools more in rural and suburban communities than in big cities.

In the next chapter we will study schools that have high poverty concentration but also high-performing students. These are the High-Poverty, High-Performing 2(HP) schools. Let us find out what the 2(HP) schools are, how they work against all odds to excel, and most important, how other schools (i.e., high or low poverty) may learn from their success.

School Type	Chicago	City	Rural	Total	%
Low poverty high performing	28	1116	506	1650	79
High poverty low performing	214	122	9	345	17
High poverty high performing	14	37	45	96	4
Low poverty low performing	0	0	0	0	0

Figure 1.5. Illinois School Types by Poverty and Performance
Source: High Poverty-High Performance (HP-HP) Schools, Illinois State Board of Education.

Chapter Two

The High-Poverty,
High-Performing 2(HP) Schools

The public school report card is a document available to the public through a state's board of education (sometimes called the state department of education or instruction) web page. Other community resources, such as real estate agencies, may also have available school information. The report card published by the state is a comprehensive one-stop shop for school information such as student demographics, student achievement, school revenue and expenditure, school staff general profile, and much more.

A quick and simple way to identify 2(HP) schools can be to study school report cards with particular focus on two important pieces of information: student demographics and student achievement.

Under student demographics is a report card section showing the percentage of students in the free and/or reduced school lunch program. Researchers use this percentage to indicate the students' social economic status. To be an eligible 2(HP) school, the percentage of students receiving free and/or reduced lunch needs to be more than 50%. This means that more than half of the student body has low social economic status or they are simply poor.

Under "student achievement" there is a report card section showing the percentage of designated grade-level students every year meeting or not meeting the state student performance requirements in reading and mathematics. To be an eligible 2(HP) school, the percentage of students meeting the state performance requirement needs to be at least 70%.

Pairing the two pieces of information, seven 2(HP) schools (five elementary schools, one middle school, and one high school) were identified across the nation. These schools from the West Coast to the East Coast are found in the states of Washington, California, Texas, Louisiana, North Carolina, Pennsylvania, and New York. To substantiate the report card information, these schools were studied to find out why the students had been high performing despite the odds of low student social economic status.

2.1. MAPLE ELEMENTARY SCHOOL— SEATTLE, WASHINGTON

A visitor entering Maple will undoubtedly notice the school's celebration of cultural diversity. In the school's reception area are clocks that tell the time in international locations including Hong Kong, London, Seoul, and Seattle. The library has a good collection of multilingual books and English-language books reflecting the many cultures of the students. The student projects that decorate the hallway also reflect cultural diversity. One display showcases students' home cooking recipes from Italian spaghetti to Southeast Asian salad rolls. The commitment to diversity is best embraced by the Maple creed that reads, "I know that our country was built by people of all races, and I know that people of all races keep our country great."

A culture of high expectations is prevalent throughout the schools and upheld by the students and school staff. Staff members work very hard to serve as role models for students. Parents often expressed that the staff are willing to take the time to focus on the children and that they are enthusiastic. Teachers are expected to help their fellow staff members and share responsibilities across grade levels so every student will be successful. "All students are our students" is the prevailing attitude reinforcing the school vision, which states, "The Maple School community of parents, staff, volunteers, and students is responsible for providing each student with the opportunity to have a positive and meaningful education in a pluralistic learning environment."

A few years ago, the Maple staff initiated a school improvement program. They began to focus on teaching the student learning standards measured by the state test. The staff worked on the different learning areas systematically. The first year they focused on math instruction, and the second year on writing skills. Writing is a foundation of Maple's curriculum. Students write every day and in every subject. As a consequence of this deliberate writing effort, students who met the state learning requirements jumped 12 percentage points in a single year. Next, the school concentrated on reading fluency and comprehension. Student achievement increased 15 percentage points. Maple's focus on teaching to the state standards had paid off.

Asked what factors make the students successful, the principal and many teachers concurred that individual student attention is the key. The staff members identified at-risk students early and worked with them so they did not fall behind. The identification of at-risk students is systematic and purposeful through the collection and analysis of student data to improve and restrategize instruction.

It is obvious that the Maple school culture and the learning elements are working beautifully due to the effective and open leadership of the principal and the leadership team. Maple's students were 63% free and/or reduced lunch. Student achievement as measured by the state test was 91% proficient in reading and 82% in mathematics.

2.2. CLARK MAGNET HIGH SCHOOL— LA CRESCENTA, CALIFORNIA

Clark is a science and technology high school focusing on college and career preparation. While all Clark students are not high achievers, the school's expectation is to make the students think they are high achievers or smart, thus giving them the confidence to do well.

Clark is a nondepartmentalized high school. The teachers integrate curriculum aligned to the California learning standards and work with students on problem-based projects. All staff and students fit nicely into the school's "can-do" culture by espousing a high level of collaboration building on trust and respect. In a sign of pride in the school, at the end of a focus group meeting, students placed their chairs neatly next to the tables, threw away the trash, and tucked in their shirts as they walked out of the library.

To assist students to reach their academic and/or career goals, two freshman courses anchor students in the science and technology path. The first foundation course is Technology Literacy, which is later followed by electives in one of four technology pathways. The second foundation course is College and Career Prep. At Clark, students prepare digital portfolios that prepare them for their high school and postsecondary plans. To reinforce their career planning, students are also required to complete at least 10 hours of community service work. Furthermore, many of the courses are industry-based certification programs with internships. As witnessed, the connection between the academics and the real world at Clark is very strong.

The instruction at Clark is data driven. All parents receive a five-week progress report from school. Student data give teachers detailed student test results based on curriculum standards and test items. A student performing below the proficient level triggers a host of interventions. Intervention strategies include differentiated instruction, peer tutoring, and supervision by the guidance department and other extra but purposeful help. The academic intervention goal of the school is to help at-risk students reach proficiency by the next marking period.

The school is one awesome learning community and the principal has the pivotal responsibility of choosing staff who have the appropriate training in the field along with an additional certification in multicultural education. More critical to selecting the right staff is the retention of the right staff before they are tenured. Clark's students were 73% free and/or reduced lunch. Student achievement as measured by the California High School Exit Examination was 84% proficient in English language arts and 90% in mathematics.

2.3. ROACH SOUTH ELEMENTARY SCHOOL—
GARLAND, TEXAS

As a history lesson begins, all eyes and ears are focused on the teacher as he reads a book about George Washington in Spanish. The teacher stops to ask questions and many hands go up. After he finishes reading, the students work in small groups to discuss the question, "Why was George Washington important in the history of the United States?" It is very clear that these second-grade students, speaking and writing in their primary language, are engaged in learning. Upon entering the school, visitors will notice that many students converse in Spanish and about half of the school's students are Limited English Proficient (LEP).

The principal of the school believes in instructing LEP students in their native language and keeping them in the program until they are proficient Spanish readers and strong in core subjects. The philosophy of the school states that early literacy instruction is achieved by the student's native language in an additive bilingualism program. The school sets out to create a learning environment where the student's first language is the language of instruction if the student is tested as deficient in English. Once those skills are proficient in the first language (this typically happens after at least three years), students begin transitioning into English instruction.

Instruction at Roach is always engaging. Teaching in all areas often starts with a basic question asking how the teacher can help the student understand what the knowledge or skill is and how it can be useful in the student's life. A teacher starts her math class by posing a problem to the class. For example, the teacher might tell the class about her new apartment house with old and ugly wallpaper. How would the teacher figure out how much new wallpaper to buy before going to the store? This obviously is an issue-oriented math problem dealing with area measurement.

Regardless of the language of instruction (Spanish or English), all students follow the same school curriculum. Two classes at the same grade level learn the same subject following an identical curriculum aligned to the prescribed Texas grade-level learning standards. Students transitioning from Spanish to English in the later grades seldom miss a beat because of the curricular consistency.

Teachers are intentional about teaching materials that are likely to appear on the state tests. They teach explicit strategies for doing well on the tests. The teaching strategy is viewed as teaching to the standards and not teaching to the test.

An extended after-school program was initially a hard sell to the parents. The program offers one hour of additional learning three afternoons a week. After the trial period, parents embraced the program as test results showed that the students in the after-school program improved their achievement.

The principal and staff alike have high expectations for all students. They believe that all students can do the work and they can do it well. Roach's students were 90% free and/or reduced lunch. Student achievement as measured by the state test was 90% proficient in reading and 100% in mathematics.

2.4. BELLE CHASSE PRIMARY SCHOOL— BELLE CHASSE, LOUSIANA

Belle Chasse starts early each day with what one might hear in a morning radio program. The student anchorpersons lead the whole school in the Pledge of Allegiance, the school motto, and "The Star-Spangled Banner"; they report on the weather and school news; and they celebrate student successes.

In a first-grade reading class, students rotate through four work stations. One group of students works with a teacher, another group reads at the computers, a third group reads independently and quietly, and the fourth group works with a teacher assistant. The teacher sets a timer for the rotation and promises that if students stay on task with no trouble, the whole class will earn points for good behavior. This class and other classes in the school run like a well-oiled machine.

Everywhere you visit, the school rules are clear and good discipline is a striking feature of Belle Chasse. Students need few reminders to stay quiet in the hallways, and they address adults as "sir" or "ma'am." All students wear blue and green uniforms, and even teachers adhere to a dress and behavior code. The school rules simply state, "Be safe; be respectful; be responsible," and even first graders can recite them by heart. Most parents support the school rules, seeing them as effective in helping the children to achieve. Classroom observations confirmed that very little teacher time is spent on disciplining students.

The sense of community is very strong in the school. Over the past years, the Belle Chasse Parent Teacher Organization has raised more than a quarter of a million dollars for various school improvement projects. Several years ago, over 500 community volunteers built a new school playground with playing and climbing structures. In 2005, Hurricane Katrina hit. The winds and flood badly damaged the school. It is a community built on trust and the leadership from the principal that brought the school through the crisis. As many parents and staff would agree, they were like a real family.

Belle Chasse has a supportive central office and a highly engaged school board. They were responsible for hiring effective staff and bringing good teaching to the children. The principal studies student data, watching for effective teachers who can model practices for other teachers, and less-successful teachers who might benefit from targeted professional development.

Belle Chasse students were 79% free and/or reduced lunch. Student achievement as measured by the state test was 78% proficient in reading and 80% in mathematics.

2.5. LAUREL HILL ELEMENTARY SCHOOL—
SCOTLAND COUNTY, NORTH CAROLINA

A parent sees two teachers standing side by side teaching in a primary classroom. The teachers chime in seamlessly that the students can really feel the power of two teachers teaching. Laurel Hill uses co-teaching to maximize the learning opportunities of general education and special education students. One teacher felt so accomplished in the team assignment that she felt more competent and that she had expanded her teaching toolbox. Co-teaching has been successful and it is one identifiable instructional strategy that one can easily observe in the classrooms.

A few years ago, students with special learning needs spent most of their instructional time in self-contained classrooms, with only limited exposure to the general education curriculum and their peers. Public reporting of student achievement showed that Laurel Hill's special education students fell behind and that kept the school from meeting the state's Adequate Yearly Progress benchmark. Consequently, the school looked for a better way of teaching students with special learning needs. The school was convinced that teaching special education students in a general education classroom (i.e., inclusive education) was the right thing to do. Subsequently, Laurel Hill's special education students exceeded the state achievement benchmark. This is a victory that did not come quickly and easily.

Teachers pointed to the principal's important role in guiding the change to inclusion education at Laurel Hill. The principal skillfully used federal and district funds to employ highly skilled and dedicated part-time teachers for core instruction. The arrangement allows for class-size reduction and small-group instruction. The principal also visits the classrooms frequently to make sure that things are going well.

Laurel Hill follows state and district guidelines with online curricula, assessments, and a pacing guide. Grade-level planning teams carefully review the instructional objectives and their alignment with the curriculum each week to ensure that all teachers address the same standards at the same time. Weekly goals and class schedules are posted outside the classroom so a visitor knows exactly what will happen during an observation.

Teachers in grades 3, 4, and 5 elect to be content (i.e., English language arts, math, science, social studies) specialists rather than elementary school teachers responsible for teaching all subjects. They divide the responsibilities of teaching. Freed from having to teach all the core subjects, teachers happily acknowledge that teaching with their strengths allows them to delve deeper into the subject content. Teachers share what they do best with their colleagues at the grade-level team meetings when students are in the special classes such as library, art, music, computers, and physical education.

Teachers at Laurel Hill are masters of routine and transitions. With students moving among groups and activities several times an hour, teachers achieve order through smooth transitions. The three basic transition commands are one clap of the hands to stand up, two claps to push in the chair, and three claps to move to the circle. Students walk the halls in near silence. They carry their supplies in tote bags provided by the school and organize their schedule with planners and note-taking books. Parents are informed about their children in school. The principal and teachers work with parents to manage problem behaviors.

In summary, Laurel Hill is driven by a culture of success to include high expectations, collaborative teaching, consistent discipline, respect, and faculty empowerment. Parents feel that there is a lot of learning besides the academics and appreciate that students are taught to be independent and to take proper responsibilities. Another parent added that the school embraces the concept of "It takes a village to educate the child."

Laurel Hill students were 76% free and/or reduced lunch. Student achievement as measured by the state test was 91% proficient in reading and 73% in mathematics.

2.6. JOSEPH E. HILL/SAMPSON L. FREEDMAN MIDDLE SCHOOL—PHILADELPHIA, PENNSYLVANIA

An examination of the grade-level curriculum surprises visitors because the classes are working one year ahead of the curriculum. Hill-Freedman's students study one grade level of academics above their peers in the school district. The purpose of teaching one year ahead is that students will feel more comfortable transitioning to high school. They will already be familiar with the materials and motivated by their success. This success will in turn encourage students to excel through high school. This in essence is Hill-Freedman's philosophy of high student expectations. The staff knows that their students can perform when pushed and encouraged. They believe that when high expectations are set, students usually meet them.

In the culture of high expectations, all students have portfolios with grades and assessment data. The portfolios are reviewed and students are expected to set new goals and expectations to be monitored by the teachers. In the fall, the counselor works with the eighth graders to identify their choices for high school. Together, they prepare portfolios with students' transcripts and assessment information. Peer-teaching is encouraged, particularly in math, giving students a feeling of self-worth. Students believe that it might be a lot of work, but no more than anyone can handle. They know that when they go to high school they will be prepared.

Whether a student's talent lies in academics, sports, or arts, he will find it at Hill-Freedman. The school offers a wide variety of extracurricular activities. The activities invite students to come and stay in school to foster learning and personal growth. The school offers 16 sports ranging from basketball, track, and soccer to tennis, golf, field hockey, and lacrosse. To participate in more than one sport, students must maintain at least a B grade point average. Besides the extracurricular instruction in dance, drama, and music, all students are involved in two annual performances: a holiday show and an end-of-the-year show.

To ensure success, the school provides an elaborate system of student support. Incoming sixth graders receive a weeklong orientation of the school's culture, rules, expectations, study skills, and team building. Sean Covey's *The 7 Habits of Highly Effective Teens* is used and discussed to keep the students focused and organized, and to help them eventually become successful. Regular student support is provided through morning homeroom advisories that help students to follow rules and address issues. Homework help and tutoring are available throughout the school year. Moreover, the school has a zero-tolerance policy for low attendance and behavior issues.

School staff responsibilities do not end at the classroom or office door. The administration instills the concept that all teachers are responsible for all students so students know they cannot play one teacher against another. The resulting culture translates to good staff communication because everyone knows everyone else in the school. At regular town hall meetings, staff, students, and parents discuss issues and resolve problems.

Hill-Freedman students were 48% free and/or reduced lunch. Eighth-grade student achievement as measured by the state test was 94% proficient in reading and 89% in mathematics.

2.7. LINCOLN ELEMENTARY SCHOOL—
MOUNT VERNON, NEW YORK

Student work is prominently displayed on the walls of the school corridors. Interestingly, the displays are not just good papers, but also artistic presentations of student work from all grades with different degrees of sophistication. The quality of displayed work emphasizes the high expectations of all students and provides a shared sense of mission. The displayed work on the walls has no signs of rips, tears, or markings; this signals a respect for the work and for fellow students. The school makes an elaborate attempt to balance academics with an infusion of arts. Capture students in the arts and the academics will follow is what the teaching staff believes. The student work display is a good reflection of discipline and respect for all in this school environment.

Instruction at Lincoln is integrated, and literacy across the curriculum is very visible. To celebrate a famous children's author, a music teacher and a first-grade teacher collaborated and taught students to read and perform a jazz rendition of Dr. Seuss's *Green Eggs and Ham*. In two fifth-grade classes, the teachers used the scientific method of investigation to propose a hypothesis, gather information, and draw a conclusion about the differences between combining an egg with green vinegar and combining an egg with green-colored water.

Science and math are frequent focuses of multidisciplinary experience. For a fifth-grade project about rocketry, students learned the difference between a dependent and independent variable by using rocket-simulating balloons to test their hypotheses about how far the balloons would travel based on their measures of inflated air volume in the balloons.

A variety of teaching strategies are in use from whole-group to small and individualized instruction. Student groupings are flexible and based on ability and interest. The school's mentoring program is available to all new and veteran teachers and to those who administrators feel may benefit from it.

At Lincoln, the leadership concurred that assessments inform instruction. Teachers said that they do not wait until a month before testing to begin to check on student academic progress. Instead, teachers administer the monthly reading and writing portfolios to measure student learning. Furthermore, teachers and specialists meet regularly to study student portfolios in order to better identify students at risk of failing. Assessment information is clearly communicated to the students and the parents or guardians through regular scheduled conferences.

A trilingual monthly newsletter helps keep the school community well informed. An active Parent Teacher Association funds and coordinates such after-school activities as reading, chess, sports, and language clubs. Parents often volunteer to help in the classrooms, and they are warmly welcomed in the school. Parents say that their children feel the caring and expectation, and consequently do not want to disappoint their teachers.

Lincoln teachers are well supported. A member of the leadership team said that there is a high level of accountability for teachers and they are given plenty of support and recognition. Many schools take teacher support for granted, and in some schools teacher support is less than adequate. At Lincoln, teachers have access to instructional supplies ready by the first day of school. How can teachers honestly complain when they have access to a copy machine on each floor of the school building?

To reach its high-performing status, Lincoln has a strong curriculum that is aligned to the state learning standards; a strong assessment system to inform instruction; a highly qualified and committed staff; a strong and supportive administrative team; and a well-informed and empowered school community.

Lincoln Elementary students were 54% free and/or reduced lunch. Fourth-grade student achievement as measured by the state test was 100% proficient in English language arts and 99% in mathematics.

2.8. THE OVERARCHING WISDOM OF THE 2(HP) SCHOOLS

What is the overarching wisdom that one can generate from the eight schools studied? Let us use inductive reasoning to see if any conclusion can be drawn from studying the 2(HP) schools. Inductive reasoning is a logic that allows for the possibility of a conclusion with the presentation of declarative premises. Let us see how inductive reasoning is employed in the following premise and concluding statement:

"The 2(HP) schools studied have effective leadership, curriculum, instruction, and assessment. Therefore, all 2(HP) schools can be generalized to have effective leadership, curriculum, instruction, and assessment."

All 2(HP) schools studied have the critical elements of leadership, curriculum, instruction, and assessment. Therefore, given the premise, the conclusion is supported. We have good reasons to accept the 2(HP) conclusion and declare that as a guide for further investigation. In chapters 3, 4, 5, and 6, we will further discuss leadership, curriculum, instruction, and assessment as success factors of the 2(HP) schools.

Chapter Three

The 2(HP) Leadership

Johnny is an elementary school teacher. He has been teaching five years in the same school with good reviews from students, parents, and the building principal. He is thinking seriously about becoming a principal in a high-need school community. Johnny knows that his career aspiration poses a professional challenge ahead of him.

He maps out a meticulous plan to prepare to become a school principal. There are three goals in the plan. The first goal is to interview a school principal intern and job shadow another school principal to better understand the real-world complexities of becoming a principal. The second goal is to survey the job market to understand the field demand and the job description. The third goal is to enroll in a university leadership certification program guided by the school administrator state standards. Johnny Brown is confident that the triangulation of the three sources of information will best prepare him to be a school principal.

3.1. WHAT ARE THE REAL-WORLD COMPLEXITIES OF *BECOMING* A SCHOOL PRINCIPAL?

Johnny interviews a Teach for America (TFA) principal intern to understand her training experience of becoming a school leader. TFA is an American nonprofit organization that recruits recent college graduates and professionals to teach for two years in low-income communities throughout the United States. The goal of TFA is for its members not only to make a short-term commitment and impact on their students, but also to become lifelong leaders in pursuing educational equality. TFA members do not have to be certified teachers, although certified teachers may apply.

In her 30s, the principal intern came into the TFA principal preparation program already with a master degree's in journalism. She is in the principal internship program and she is getting ready to take on her own school. Young, and willing to do things out of the box, she has a lot in common with many of the upcoming new principals in the school system.

The intern is highly skillful in using technology and data analysis. These traits are not only common but required among school principals nowadays. Data skills will be a part of the required assessments under the state's principal preparation programs. Needing to know that the work you are doing is quantifiable is important in the job description of a school principal. Hence in many school systems across the country, being data savvy is becoming a key component of the principal's tool kit linked to performance management and instructional improvement. Johnny notes that the one very important task the intern accomplished over the summer break involved data analysis and strategizing.

The intern helped teachers organize their curricula, allowing them to understand the important alignment of student learning to the state learning standards and assessments. The intern works closely with the school principal and gets hands-on experience in all aspects of the job from dawn to dusk. These experiences include welcoming students first thing in the morning and seeing them off at the end of the school day. The intern is in and out of meetings with staff, parents, and students almost on a continuous basis; she conducts lunchroom and playground supervision (including defusing fights); she visits classrooms and teachers; she leads and facilitates school committees of all sorts; and she meets and discusses issues with central office staff and school community leaders.

When the intern completes the Teach for America's principal preparation program and is offered a job, she will be required to spend four years working as an administrator in a traditional school (as opposed to a charter school) in the system. What Johnny learns from the intern is that to be a principal means hard work and top commitment to run the school.

3.2. WHAT ARE THE REAL-WORLD COMPLEXITIES OF *BEING* A SCHOOL PRINCIPAL?

Johnny is meticulous in selecting a school principal whom he would like to job shadow. He wants to pick effective school leaders in high-need communities. Johnny used the public school report card to pick Jefferson Elementary School in New York. Jefferson's students were 98.3% low income and they met the state reading and mathematics proficiency requirement for two consecutive years from 2007 to 2009.

The principal at Jefferson already held one meeting before the first school bell. He greeted the students in a mix of English and Spanish and reminded them to be on time and not to leave trash on the floor. As the bell rang the principal swept into a classroom. The class began with silent reading as the teacher wrote the lesson objective on the board. The principal kept walking around the class, observing students over their shoulders, quietly asking questions, and carefully taking notes. The principal on a typical day will visit at least two classes and meet with teachers to discuss their teaching performance. He will also meet with staff members to discuss the improvement of school programs with the analysis of school improvement data. Last but not least, he will meet with students and parents for various discipline issues.

It is obvious to Johnny that the principal wears many hats, including chief executive officer, student advocate, instructional leader, social worker, staff supporter and supervisor, school improvement manager, and leader in the community. On top of all the responsibilities, the principal is usually praised if student achievement goes up and blamed if it goes down. Johnny's opinion is that being a school principal is one of the

tenured but ineffective teachers. Due to the high accountability and challenges, the turnover rates for school principals have increased because the principals are tired and stressed.

Today's new principals have less teaching experience compared to their predecessors a decade ago. Nowadays, more top education administrators could be coming from other nonteaching professions. For example, Ron Huberman, the immediate past chief executive officer of Chicago Public Schools, is formally trained in the field of social work and business. He served as a police officer before his appointment. Paul Vallas is currently the school superintendent in the Recovery School District in Louisiana. He is formally trained in the field of political science and history. He served previously as the budget director of the city of Chicago. Arne Duncan, currently the U.S. secretary of education, previously ran a nonprofit education organization in Chicago.

Many new principals often land their first job in a low-performing school. In contrast, experienced principals are clustered more in higher-performing schools. Unfortunately, moving up the career ladder sometimes means leaving a low-performing school for one that is high performing and easier to work in. A change in school leadership can throw off any school improvement efforts.

In a big-city school system like Chicago, principal candidates need to clear the hurdle of a principal examination that gauges the applicant's ability to handle real-life scenarios. Here is a sample question from the principal examination (Baser and Harris 2010).

One of your veteran teachers is going through a difficult divorce and as the principal, you have observed a recent change in his performance. He frequently takes days off and is often late to school. His students are not performing as well on interim assessments and other measures of student progress as they have in the past. Though he has been consistently high-performing in the past, you are worried about the impact on students.

What action would you most likely take first?

1. Because he is one of your best teachers, leave the situation alone as it will probably resolve itself over time.
2. Meet with a teacher who is close to this person and ask the person to talk to the teacher and help him through this difficult time.
3. Meet with the teacher to offer your assistance, set expectations for his attendance and student progress, and mutually agree on a follow-up plan.
4. Discuss with the teacher that his behavior is harmful to students and will require immediate corrective action.
5. Move him to a different classroom where his attendance may not be an issue.

Which answer option demonstrates that a candidate recognizes the need to take responsibility for resolving issues, to hold himself and others accountable for meeting performance standards, to set expectations for staff, and to build and maintain an effective school team? The correct answer is 3.

3.4. WHAT ARE THE STATE LICENSURE
REQUIREMENTS OF SCHOOL LEADERSHIP?

There is no single career path to prepare a person to become an education leader; Huberman, Vallas, and Duncan, who are previously discussed, are good examples. Nevertheless, a person like Johnny who aspires to be a school principal should seek relevant roles and experiences (i.e., classroom teacher), that help him to acquire the competencies required for success, that is, knowledge, skills, and attitude.

Many universities across the country use the Interstate School Leaders Licensure Consortium (ISLLC) standards to develop their leadership programs and prepare candidates for the state licensure examination. There are six standards:

1. A school administrator is an educational leader who promotes the success of all students by *facilitating the development, articulation, implementation, and stewardship of a vision of learning that is shared and supported by the school community.*
2. A school administrator is an educational leader who promotes the success of all students by *advocating, nurturing, and sustaining a school culture and instructional program conducive to student learning and staff professional growth.*
3. A school administrator is an educational leader who promotes the success of all students by *ensuring management and organization, operations, and resources for a safe, efficient, and effective learning environment.*
4. A school administrator is an educational leader who promotes the success of all students by *collaborating with families and community members, responding to diverse community interests and needs, and mobilizing community resources.*
5. A school administrator is an educational leader who promotes the success of all students by *acting with integrity, fairness, and in an ethical manner.*
6. A school administrator is an educational leader who promotes the success of all students by *understanding, responding to, and influencing the larger political, social, economic, legal, and cultural context.*

Are you a visionary leader? Do you have a vision burning inside that seeks to manifest itself? A visionary leader is good with words as well as with actions. A visionary leader is effective in manifesting his or her vision because he or she creates specific, achievable goals, initiates action, and more important, enlists the participation of others. Talk and discuss issues with school leaders who you know are regarded as effective. Analyze the pattern of the thinking based on the conversation. Do you find their thinking broad and systematic? Do they have a big picture of things, the whole system, and the pattern that connects? Visionary leaders embody a balance of right brain (rational) and left brain (intuitive) functions. To be a visionary school leader, in essence, is what standard 1 is about.

"I have not been to a workshop for five years, and I do not plan to start now." This is what one teacher says in the teachers' lounge. The teacher reflects on the unsupportive culture of the administration for professional development. *"I have presented in a reading technology conference and the principal asked me to be the trainer of*

reading technology on the next professional development day." This is what a teacher says in another school. The teacher demonstrates that her school encourages, celebrates, and reinforces the importance of professional development. The two teachers contrast the unwritten rules about how to behave, and that is an important part of the school culture.

The culture of a school is a key factor in productivity and success. Culture affects the willingness of students, staff members, parents, and administrators to put in the time for continuous improvement. Without such a culture, changes and improvement will simply not happen. Shaping a school culture starts with the school leader. The school principal shapes the culture in or his or her day-to-day interactions with people. The daily work of the school principal is a great opportunity to reinforce or change the culture. Every interaction with a student, a staff member, or a parent is a chance to do and show that. To shape a positive and productive school culture, in essence, is what standard 2 is about.

A few years ago a school principal was on a flight from Chicago to Cincinnati. He had nothing to read but *The One Minute Manager*, by Kenneth Blanchard and Spencer Johnson. It was written in 1982 and still sells very well today, according to its Amazon.com ranking. It was a short flight, and an easy book to read. The reader came down to this summary at the end of reading the book:

The effective manager makes specific expectations. Tell people what is expected. Follow through. Track results. Tell people afterward how they did. Set new expectations and repeat process if needed.

Education is a business working with people. To manage a learning environment effectively, the principal needs to know how to get the job done through leading people to higher productivity and the greater good of the organization. To create and manage a productive school environment for learning is, in essence, what standard 3 is about.

To be an effective school leader, the principal needs to have a supportive environment. A school principal may define the parents, faculty, and staff as his environment. This environment may extend to the entire school community to define his territory of support. The principal collaborates with people to make decisions, and he often engages in politics. In a broad sense, any human group interactions involving a power struggle can be described as politics.

Manage your government correctly at the start of the war.
Close your borders and tear up passports.
Block the passage of envoys.
Encourage politicians at headquarters to stay out of it.
You must use any means to put an end to politics.

(Sunzi 2003, chap. 11)

As Sun Tzu reveals in *The Art of War*, unneeded politics need to stay clear of effective management. The school leader works with politics, and sometimes dirty politics. One veteran school administrator advises aspirants to stay out of school leadership if they do not like working with people or dealing with school politics.

Creating a professional learning community is a collective method of effective leadership from the principal. To work collaboratively with the community to build consensus, is, in essence, what standard 4 is about.

Imagine you are sitting by a swimming pool when a small child begins to drown. The lifeguard is nowhere to be found. What would you do? It depends. Can you swim? It would be foolish to jump in if you cannot swim, and there is a difference between being brave and being foolish. Would you save the child if he or she were somebody else's child, or your own? This scenario provides an interesting glimpse into how we uphold the moral law, ethics, and integrity. What we know is that people are usually more than willing to sacrifice if they see the worthiness of the cause.

As a school principal, how would you set and uphold moral standards for yourself as a leader and your organization, the school? What constitutes the moral purpose of a school can be described by answering the following questions:

1. What is the primary purpose of a school?
2. What does a school represent?
3. Why did you enter the education profession?
4. Why do you aspire to become a school principal?

The intention of these questions is to cause reflection on self-meaning (as a leader) and organizational meaning (as a school). A careful examination of these questions will give us a sense of moral purpose as leaders working in education. To work as an ethical and fair school leader is, in essence, what standard 5 is about.

Let us examine a hypothetical school community with five interest groups. They serve different needs confronting issues and challenges. The first is a local community service club that has been having trouble recruiting members and volunteers for the past few years. The second is a state youth congress that represents school leaders from around the state, and youth violence is a focus of the congress's platform. The third is a parent-teacher organization facing increases in delinquency, truancy, and illegal drug use among teens. The fourth is a community action group in an economically deprived, ethnically diverse neighborhood. Last, the fifth is a YMCA that has just received a grant with a focus on school-community partnerships for youth.

As a school leader, how would you motivate the five groups and work with them to address the community issues and benefit students? What if you have the opportunity to get extra school funding? How would you analyze a funding proposal framework (figure 3.1) to pull the community groups together to achieve healthy youth behaviors? How can the five community groups be the stakeholders? How can they use their expertise and contribute to the common good of the community to promote youth health?

An effective school leader recognizes the importance of establishing good partnership with the larger school community—parents, businesses, government agencies, and other institutions. He or she strives to develop the community allegiance to and ownership of the school. It is the collective work and responsibility of the entire school community that will influence the degree to which all children are successful. It is imperative that the community participate meaningfully in school governance and deci-

Goal: to attain healthy behaviors
for all children and youth

Start: set healthy beliefs and standards...
in families, schools, community

Build: bonding such as attachment and commitment
... to families, schools, community

Provide: opportunities, skills, recognition...
in families, school, communities

Nurture: individual characteristics and behaviors

Figure 3.1.   Community Health Promotion Project Proposal
Source: Courtesy of the author.

sion making. In that sense, this can be done through the school board of education with elected representatives from the community. Such a partnership demonstrates a relationship in which different community representations (i.e., business, government, etc.) bring specific skills and expertise to the school, offer a different perspective on issues, offer support in difficult times, and contribute to the achievement of common goals.

In summary, the ISLLC standard statements all start with, "A school administrator is an educational leader who promotes the success of all students" to reinforce the centrality and importance of student learning in school leadership. The roles of the school leaders have changed from the traditional role of working only in the school building to being an extension of the school community. The power of school leadership moves from the office of the principal to the constituents of the community. The effectiveness of leadership is performance based with quantifiable accountability. Last, the ISLLC standards are predicated on the concepts of accessibility, opportunity, empowerment, and performance of all stakeholders in the school community.

You have learned the essential elements of effective school leaders. Can you identify similar leadership elements of the 2(HP) described in chapter 2 to see how they bring about high student success?

REFERENCES

Blanchard, K., and S. Johnson. 1982. *The one minute manager*. New York: Morrow.

Baser, D., and R. Harris. 2010. Candidate pool shrinks. *Catalyst Chicago*, Spring.

Gates S., et al. 2003. *Who is leading our schools? An overview of school administrators and their careers*. Santa Monica, CA: RAND.

Sunzi. 2003. *The art of war plus the ancient Chinese revealed*. Trans. G. Gagliardi. Seattle: Clearbridge.

Does the textbook provide the teachers with what they need rather than want? In order to appeal to a wide consumer market, textbook publishers usually provide more than teachers can possibly teach. Select the most important knowledge and skills and focus on the quality of student understanding rather than on the quantity of information presented. What have we learned from Judy in the previous section regarding how she used the textbook to make careful curriculum decisions? The textbook is only a reference point of the curriculum; it alone is not the curriculum.

4.2. WHAT IS A GRADE-LEVEL CURRICULUM?

At the beginning of the chapter, we looked at the purposeful efforts going into planning a lesson. These efforts reflect decisions about the curriculum. What is a curriculum? Educational theorists offer a wide variety of curriculum definitions. Some common definitions (Ornstein and Hunkins 2004) include a blueprint of learning; a course of study; the planned educational experiences of a school; and the process used by teachers to select and organize student-learning experiences.

Judy wanted her students to understand that graphs help us represent information (data); therefore, her lesson goal was the result of that deliberate curriculum decision. Here, we will simply define curriculum as everything that teachers teach and students learn in schools.

When we define the curriculum as "everything that teachers teach and students learn in schools," we do not limit that definition to only the content of each lesson. Instead, we are referring more broadly to the knowledge, skills, and attitudes that students learn in school. How do curricula impart knowledge, skills, and attitude?

Analyze the following typical schedule of an elementary school teacher (figure 4.2). How are the learning experiences organized throughout the day? What is taught in the elementary school curriculum?

Time	Activities
8:30 AM	School starts
8:30-8:45	Morning announcement
8:45-10:30	English language arts
10:30-11:20	Mathematics
11:20-11:50	Lunch
11:50-12:20	Story time
12:20-1:15	Learning center time (practice language arts and math)
1:15-1:45	Physical education/supervised activities
1:45-2:30	Science/social science
2:30-2:45	Afternoon announcement
2:45-3:00	Dismissal

Figure 4.2. Elementary School Schedule
Source: Courtesy of the author.

In a typical school day, the elementary teacher spends approximately 105 minutes teaching language arts (i.e., listening, speaking, reading, writing, spelling), and an additional 30 minutes reading stories. The teacher spends 70 minutes on mathematics and splits 75 minutes between science and social science. In elementary school, physical education, music, and arts are taught by special teachers, and in the schedule 30 minutes are devoted to that. It is more than obvious that English language arts and mathematics are the top two curriculum priorities of the schedule. Science and social science receive secondary attention. It is not a coincidence that the schedule priorities align with the reading and mathematics priorities of the No Child Left Behind mandate as seen in the 2(HP) schools studied in chapter 2.

Let us visit a middle school. A middle school differs from a junior high school in its philosophy of teaching adolescents through integration in lieu of departmentalizing the subject areas. Three middle school teachers discuss how they plan to prepare a series of lessons across the subject areas. Joan is a sixth-grade social science teacher in a middle school. She and her grade level team have a common planning period twice a week. During the planning period, the team members talk to one another about the teaching successes and challenges that they share with the same group of students. Analyze the following conversation between the teachers. How are the learning experiences developed? What is emphasized in the middle school curriculum?

Joan, the social science teacher, says, "*I will be teaching the Civil War unit in two weeks. At the conclusion of the unit, each student group will have to make a report. Are there ways that this Civil War unit can connect with what you will be doing in the curriculum?*"

Jim, the English language arts teacher, offers, "*I could have the students read Crane's* The Red Badge of Courage. *The book is on the district's reading list and should do a good job of communicating the realities of the Civil War.*"

"*That would be great,*" Joan answers. "*This is what the students need to know—something to help them understand that history is about people and time. How about you, Jeremy? Are there any teaching connections to mathematics?*"

"*We are working on statistics in mathematics right now. I can find old Civil War data such as the number of free colored persons, slaveholders, households owning slaves and more to illustrate how different kinds of data fit with different kinds of graphs. Students can include different kinds of graphs in their reports,*" says Jeremy, the mathematics teacher.

The rationale of cross-curricular planning is that there is a greater emphasis on content; students need experts in various content areas (English language arts, social science, and mathematics in our scenario above) to challenge them. Unlike in elementary schools, the content areas are each allocated the same amount of instructional time. The middle school curriculum emphasizes real-life situations and attempts to connect more to the interests of the students.

The curriculum in a junior high school and a high school is less integrated by nature. The teaching focus is on separate disciplines, and the area of learning becomes more specialized and, some say, more fragmented. A typical high school freshman may study English from 9:20 to 10:10, then algebra from 10:15 to 11:05, and so on through the rest of the day. People argue that dividing the curriculum into compartments is isolated learning and it bears little resemblance to the real world outside the school. Instead, schools should offer an integrated curriculum in which concepts and skills from various disciplines are connected and reinforced. Interestingly, the integrated curriculum strategies were what we saw in many of the 2(HP) schools studied in chapter 2.

4.3. WHY ARE EXTRACURRICULAR ACTIVITIES IMPORTANT?

A school board approves a drastic budget slash to reduce the number of sports and clubs. What the school board does not quite understand is that extracurricular activities such as sports and clubs provide positive outlets for students. They are an essential part of the student's total school experience. Researchers (Fredericks and Eccles 2006) claim that extracurricular activities actually reduce school dropout rates and delinquent behavior, and increase academic success. Unfortunately, at-risk students who can benefit most from the extracurricular activities are less likely to participate, further alienating themselves from the school.

One 2(HP) student honestly reveals, *"If it is not for the after-school basketball games I will not even come to school."* Although outside the formal academic curriculum, extracurriculum provides undeniably valuable learning experiences and student self-esteem. We find that well-developed extracurricular programs are an integral support of the 2(HP) school successes.

4.4. WHAT ARE THE MISSION AND VISION OF A SCHOOL CURRICULUM?

The most important question in any organization has to be, "What is the business of our business?" Answering this question is the first step in setting priorities.

—Judith Bardwick (1996, 134)

The curriculum creates a blueprint for the subsequent instruction-assessment process. The development of a curriculum, which culminates in a written document, takes expertise, collaboration, and time. The document guides the school to ensure that board policy and district administrative rules are followed. There are several components in the curriculum; the first two important ones are the mission and the vision.

Mission and vision are two confusing items in business lingo because they are often used interchangeably to build the foundation of an organization. Vision statements and mission statements are power-packed drivers in a workplace's culture. They are used to release the potential energy within the people working in the organization. The best missions and visions become mantras for action. The worst ones are those pretty, carefully crafted, long, and detailed ones up on the walls in frames: there is too much to memorize and remember, or too much to bother with at all, or no one pays attention to them, and no one lives them. Mission and vision matter only if people use them.

The mission challenges members of an organization to reflect on the purpose of its existence—the business of the business! It answers the question of why are we doing what we are doing in the first place instead of how are we going to do better.

Here is a generalized mission statement of a 2(HP) school. "It is our job to create a conducive school environment that engages students in academic learning that results in a high level of achievement. We are confident that with our support, students can master challenging curricula, and we expect them to do so. We are prepared to work collaboratively with students, colleagues, and parents to achieve this shared educational purpose."

While many schools believe that every student can learn, they might respond to the charge in different ways. Effective schools must go beyond the clichés to look at their mission of education. Instead, they must take the challenge by the "horns" to answer the tougher questions that address the heart of the business of education: What do we expect our students to learn? And how do we realize learning for all students?

Whereas a mission gives a purpose to an organization, vision instills an organization with direction. A good vision statement gives a clear picture of the organization's future. It is a compelling statement that members of the school community are motivated to make a reality. Here is a generalized vision of the 2(HP) school regarding its stance on curriculum. The 2(HP) school believes:

1. Curriculum development is a participatory process involving major stakeholders representing grade levels and subject matter specialty.
2. The written curriculum is a document that cannot be compromised. It serves the learning needs of all students.
3. The curriculum is responsive to social technological changes through a regular and systematic review process.
4. The school holds itself accountable for providing needed resources to implement the written curriculum; teachers are responsible for delivering the curriculum; students are responsible for learning; and parents are responsible for supporting their children in pursuing an education. Accountability rests in all school constituents.

4.5. WHAT IS THE STANDARDS-BASED APPROACH TO CURRICULUM DEVELOPMENT?

Standards-based curriculum is driven by the establishment of academic standards for what students should know and be able to do. These standards are used to guide all other system components. The standards-based process calls for clear, measurable standards for all students. Rather than norm-referenced rankings, a standards-based system measures each student against the concrete standard instead of measuring how well the student performed compared to others. Please note that the 2(HP) school curricula are all aligned to the state learning standards with no exceptions. For that reason, the alignment of the school curriculum to the state learning standards is not optional to high student achievement.

The development of a standards-based curriculum is very time consuming. It takes a group of dedicated professionals working together to create a blueprint for teaching and learning. Study the process below and examine the creation of the product—the curriculum.

1. Assemble a committee of teachers to review and develop the curriculum standards of a selected subject area such as English language arts, mathematics, science, or social sciences. The selection of the committee members is crucial and often political. Selected members of the committee should be well respected in the profession, well regarded in their field of expertise, and well represented across the grade levels. Imagine how a teacher might react or even follow a guide that is developed by someone who is not well respected or an expert in his or her field of instruction. The teachers' union president (assuming that he or she has instructional duties in the classroom), grade level lead teachers, and department chairs are usually good choices.
2. Review and analyze carefully the state goals and standards frameworks that teachers are obligated to follow. The committee should reference official documents where the state says what should be learned and assessed at grade levels. Student learning standards vary from state to state. State standards documents are usually lengthy and complicated. The standards should be clearly distinguished from goals and benchmarks (see figure 4.3). For all practical purposes, the state assessment is standards driven and that is why the curriculum needs to align to the state learning standards.
3. Break the frameworks down into specific knowledge and skills that each student should be able to accomplish in a measurable learning objective. This is the first step of the standard alignment process. Failure to align to standards will lead to teachers' not teaching on targets and eventually lead students away from the intended learning goals.
4. Begin each knowledge or skill objective with "Students will be able to . . . " For example: "Students will be able to count from 1 to 10 without using their fingers" or "Students will be able to write a lead sentence to introduce the ideas of the paragraph." The essence of steps 3 and 4 is to answer the question, "What educational purposes should the school seek to attain?"
5. Develop lesson plans and activities that will teach the knowledge skill of the standards-based curriculum in a style that engages the learning styles of the students. It is in step 5 that curriculum can be developed to achieve curriculum differentiation. A differentiated curriculum is one that is individualized to meet the diverse needs of all the students in the class. As one gifted-education teacher in a 2(HP) school says, "*Equity means giving everyone equal opportunities to learn, not teaching everyone in exactly the same way.*" If implemented appropriately, differentiation does not have to mean more work for the teacher. In fact, it will allow a teacher to spend his or her time more efficiently with a greater number of students. Step 5 is often taken closely with teaching because differentiation manifests itself in both curriculum and instruction.
6. Organize and sequence the learning objectives into different levels of progressing complexity from low to high grades. Some of the concepts and/or skills are introduced, taught, and reinforced at specific grade levels or with specific reference to the intended outcome of the program, course, unit, and lesson. For example, an early elementary student is expected to describe an observation in science. A late elementary student is expected to formulate questions on a specific science topic

STATE GOAL 1: Read with understanding and fluency.

Why This Goal is important. Reading is essential. It is the process by which people gain information and ideas from books, newspapers, manuals, letters, contracts, advertisements and a host of other materials. Using strategies for constructing meaning before, during and after reading will help students connect what they read now with what they have learned in the past. Students who read well and widely build a strong foundation for learning in all areas of life.

→ *STANDARD*

A. Apply word analysis and vocabulary skills to comprehend selections. →

EARLY ELEMENTARY	LATE ELEMENTARY	MIDDLE/JUNIOR HIGH SCHOOL	EARLY HIGH SCHOOL	LATE HIGH SCHOOL
1.A.1a Apply word analysis skills (e.g., phonics, word patterns) to recognize new words.	**1.A.2a** Read and comprehend unfamiliar words using root words, synonyms, antonyms, word origins and derivations.	**1.A.3a** Apply knowledge of word origins and derivations to comprehend words used in specific content areas (e.g., scientific, political, literary, mathematical).	**1.A.4a** Expand knowledge of word origins and derivations and use idioms, analogies, metaphors and similes to extend vocabulary development.	**1.A.5a** Identify and analyze new terminology applying knowledge of word origins and derivations in a variety of practical settings.
1.A.1b Comprehend unfamiliar words using context clues and prior knowledge; verify meanings with resource materials.	**1.A.2b** Clarify word meaning using context clues and a variety of resources including glossaries, dictionaries and thesauruses.	**1.A.3b** Analyze the meaning of words and phrases in their context.	**1.A.4b** Compare the meaning of words and phrases and use analogies to explain the relationships among them.	**1.A.5b** Analyze the meaning of abstract concepts and the effects of particular word and phrase choices.

BENCHMARK

Figure 4.3. Goals, Standards, and Benchmarks

Mathematics

(Elementary School level)

Measurement and Estimation

STATE STANDARD: Measure and compare quantities using appropriate units, instruments, and methods.

The learner will be able to...	Time	Strand	Resources
• Measure the length and width of a rectangle such as a piece of paper or a table using a metric ruler to the nearest meter.	...days/weeks	Length	Textbook... Web sites... Other........
• Measure and calculate two dimensional figures using a metric ruler to the nearest centimeter.	...days/weeks	Area	Textbook... Web sites... Other........
• Measure and calculate three dimensional figures using a metric ruler to the nearest millimeter.	...days/weeks	Volume	Textbook... Web sites... Other........

Figure 4.5. Mathematics Curriculum
Source: Courtesy of the author.

English Language Arts

(Elementary School level)

Writing

<u>STATE STANDARD</u>: Compose well-organized and coherent writing for specific purposes and audiences.

The learner will be able to...	<u>Time</u>	<u>Strand</u>	<u>Resources</u>
• Use pre-writing strategies to generate and organize ideas to include a beginning, a middle, and an end. Use descriptive words when writing about people, things, and events.	...days/weeks	Pre-writing	Textbook... Web sites... Other.........
• Use a variety of pre-writing strategies such as mapping, outlining, drafting. Support main ideas with at least one example in different purpose compositions.	...days/weeks	Pre-writing Writing	Textbook... Web sites... Other.........

Figure 4.6. English Language Arts Curriculum
Source: Courtesy of the author.

Science

(Elementary School level)

Scientific Inquiry

STATE STANDARD: Know and apply the concepts, principles and processes of scientific inquiry.

The learner will be able to...	Time	Strand	Resources
• Observe and describe an event in the physical world or the natural world using qualitative and quantitative words.	...days/weeks	Observation	Textbook... Web sites... Other.........
• Develop questions on an observation that are related to scientific topics.	...days/weeks	Questioning	Textbook... Web sites... Other.........
• Collect and record data for investigations related to science topics.	...days/weeks	Data collection Data recording	Textbook... Web sites... Other.........
• Interpret data for investigations related to science topics.	...days/weeks	Data Interpretation	Textbook... Web sites... Other.........

Figure 4.7. Science Curriculum
Source: Courtesy of the author.

Social Science

(Elementary School level)

Shaping Forces of History

STATE STANDARD: Understand events, trends individuals and movements shaping the history of the state, the nation, and the world.

The learner will be able to....	Time	Strand	Resources
• Explain the difference between past, present, and future time.	...days/weeks	Time in History	Textbook... Web sites... Other........
• Describe and compare people and events in past, present and future time.	...days/weeks	People in History	Textbook... Web sites... Other........
• Read selected historical stories to determine the significance and the impact.	...days/weeks	Historical events and the impact	Textbooks... Web sites... Other........
• Compare different historical stories to understand the perspectives they represent.	...days/weeks	Historical Analysis	Textbooks... Web sites... Other........

Figure 4.8. Social Science Curriculum
Source: Courtesy of the author.

Chapter Five

The 2(HP) Instruction

"My students are not convinced about the importance of health risks. They are too young. They still have not gone through enough life experiences to understand the consequences of health risks," says Irene, a science teacher.

"Health risks?" asks Hung, another science teacher sharing an office with Irene.

"My students had trouble understanding the how living things function, adapt and change questions in the state test last year. I try to use more concrete, real-world examples. I want my students to be more engaged in the learning. I need to go beyond the textbook and provide students with more learning reinforcement," says Irene.

"I have a good friend working in the hospital. I can ask her for some retired health records. You can study and modify the records, white out the patient's name and other personal confidential information. Will that be real world enough for your students?" says Hung, genuinely interested.

"Sounds like a plan," Irene thinks as Hung leaves the room hurriedly for his next class.

Like Irene, many teachers develop and refine their professional knowledge and skills, with the ultimate goal of delivering effective lessons. If we look closely at Irene's planning, we see that her understanding of the ways that students engage were important in guiding her decisions to plan and teach well.

Behind the teaching of effective lessons are the principles of learning. These principles explain learning by emphasizing changes in the ways learners think that result from their efforts to connect. The purpose of first understanding the principles is to connect them later to effective teaching strategies that we will describe in this chapter. Teaching strategies can be explained using a tree analogy. The strategies draw from the learning principles, like the tree roots taking nutrients from the soil. The nutrients then go up the tree trunk and the branches to sustain the leaves; this represents the manifestation of various effective teaching strategies. The success of the many 2(HP) teaching strategies we saw in chapter 2 is grounded in the following six basic principles of learning.

1. Learners thrive in a supportive environment.
2. Learners connect to prior knowledge.
3. Learners construct knowledge.

4. Learning needs regular feedback and practice.
5. Learning requires experience.
6. Learning is enhanced by social interaction.

5.1. LEARNERS THRIVE IN A SUPPORTIVE ENVIRONMENT

Classroom management consists of practices and procedures that a teacher uses to maintain an environment in which instruction and learning can occur. For this to happen, the teacher must have a well-ordered environment.

—Harry K. Wong (2001)

"Teaching is not about talking knowledgeably!" says an education professor on the first day of an education foundation class. *"You need more than just subject-matter expertise to help you to become an effective teacher,"* adds the professor. *"The fact that you have a college degree in English does not make you an English teacher. You need to provide students with a supportive learning environment to include managing the learning resources, dealing with students, and a host of other things."* The class looks on with great interest. *"You will not be able to teach if the class is not well managed. A classroom that is not well managed is inviting confusion and programming students to fail. The management of the physical environment of a class and the mental environment of the students are equally important,"* the professor continues.

Visit a school in your neighborhood. Walk the hallway to feel the ambience of the school. Look through the window of the classroom door without interrupting the class. Are the students learning and the teacher teaching? Compare teacher effectiveness by looking at classroom management and see whether students are on task learning. Almost all surveys of teacher effectiveness report that classroom management skills are crucial in determining the establishment of a supportive learning environment. For students to be on task learning, the environment must be conducive both physically and mentally. Students are expected to pay attention, be respectful, be cooperative, and be motivated to learn. For the teacher to achieve that goal, the classroom must have a positive climate that includes adequate, accessible, well-organized materials for productive work.

A supportive learning environment includes a place that is physically clean, well organized, and welcoming. We will not go into the details of physically preparing a classroom because it reflects the personal taste of the person doing it. Remember, when students see piles of homework on the teacher's desk, the piles can be perceived as "there is no hurry to turn in work on time because the teacher is behind in grading homework." When students see a wall with diplomas and certificates, that can be perceived as "the teacher is showing his credentials and demands respect." When students see the teacher's desk with leftover meals from the day before, that can be perceived as "the teacher eats and works at the desk; the teacher is sloppy."

In addition to teaching, the teacher needs to fulfill other nonteaching duties equally effectively. What will the teacher do to dismiss the class, when students are disruptive, a child calls in sick for the day, a student needs to go to the nurse's office, another child needs a tissue to blow his nose, a student comes in dressed inappropriately and having left his projects at home, and the list goes on. The situations previously described can be handled quite adequately if the teacher knows and enforces the class rules and school policies.

Do you know that it is a part of the teacher's job description to know and enforce school rules? School rules are in the school handbook, and it is simply the interpretation of the school laws. A teacher can run into legal issues and worse yet, lose his job when the laws are not interpreted and enforced correctly. Figure 5.1 is a section from the Flat Rock Elementary School (South Carolina) handbook with reference to discipline rules. The various ways the teacher handles the different classroom situations contributes significantly to the environment of the class, and that is not even related to whether the room is clean or the student desks are placed in orderly rows.

Flat Rock Elementary School

"Where Character Rocks"

DISCIPLINE

The teachers and staff at Flat Rock Elementary School strive to provide the best possible education for students. Discipline is a cooperative effort among students, parents, teachers, and administrators. In order to produce the best environment, it is necessary that all students demonstrate appropriate cooperation and respect toward teachers, substitutes, and staff members. **Classroom misbehavior is not acceptable.**

1. Students must show respect toward others at all times. It is expected that language directed towards teachers and fellow students will be polite and appropriate.
2. Disrespect for those in authority will be reason for severe action.
3. Staff members of the school are responsible for the supervision of all students. Students must obey and respect every member of the staff, whether or not they are under their direct supervision. Directions by teachers, substitutes, and other members of the school staff must be followed. A student may disagree with the directions of the school staff but does not have the right to disobey the direct and reasonable instruction of a teacher.
4. The Anderson County District Three Discipline Code will be enforced. A parent conference, detention, and suspensions are not considered too severe for the school to take in order to maintain an atmosphere which will lead to a good education. **We expect our students to be well-mannered and considerate of others.**
5. Weapons (knives, guns, swords, or other similar items) are not allowed.
6. Bullying is unacceptable behavior.

Figure 5.1.   The School Handbook (Flat Rock Elementary)
Source: Used with permission from Flat Rock Elementary. www.anderson3.k12.sc.us/flat_rock/handbook.html

Effective schools critically run on high student expectations (Edmonds 1977). Demonstrated high expectations are not only for all students but for staff as well. The belief is that students are capable and able to learn and that teachers are capable of making it happen. A teacher, through his classroom management skills, can demonstrate the high expectations for all students to be successful.

How does a teacher share his high expectations for students? The effective teacher sets clear expectations right from the beginning to avoid student misunderstanding. Here is how Ms. Rodriguez, a high school English teacher, welcomes her class.

"Good morning and welcome to an exciting new school term. My name is Ms. Rodriguez and it is already written on the white board. I am excited to be your English teacher and I have been teaching in this school for six years. I am an keen reader of professional journals. I love to write and currently I am finishing a book on comparative literature. I hope my professional activities will motivate you to do well in this class. I guarantee that you will have one of the most unforgettable learning experiences in your high school career. We will learn about writing and other important life skills that will help you to be successful in college. I am confident that if you should run into me at the supermarket 20 years from now, you will say that Ms. Rodriguez's class was exciting and most memorable. So welcome aboard!"

In this brief welcoming speech, Ms. Rodriguez introduces herself as a lifelong learner driven by her interests and professional activities. Note how the teacher shares her passion for learning and interests in the subject matter because this attitude can be contagious. The part that says, *"Motivate you to do well in class . . . will help you to be successful in college"* is setting high expectations that all students will do well and go to college after graduation.

Ms. Rodriguez's success may have already been determined because of her fine reputation of creating a supportive environment for her students. If you are committed to an environment of high expectations for all students, the students will come to your class with high expectations; this will result in an enjoyable and successful school year for everyone.

Another very important aspect of creating a supportive learning environment is the use of instructional technology and resources. *"I used to teach my class bare knuckles, and now I can't do it well without the use of assistive education technology,"* said a veteran teacher. *"For one thing, how can I split myself among 26 students and cater to their learning needs? I can now individualize my instruction with technology and go beyond the four walls of the classroom,"* the teacher continued. The use of education technology is becoming indispensable in effective teaching, and this is evident in the 2(HP) schools in chapter 2 using creative state and federal financing to procure the equipment. Some common uses of technology are the computer labs, calculators, and distance learning.

5.2. LEARNERS CONNECT TO PRIOR KNOWLEDGE

In a scene from the movie *The Sound of Music*, the governess Maria (played by Julie Andrews) takes the seven Von Trapp children on a bike ride. As they ride, some children follow Maria, some ride alongside Maria, and some ride ahead. One child is too young to ride and she is carried on Maria's back. If Maria is to teach the children how to ride bicycles and assume that they do not know how, then she will be in for a surprise. To assume the learners have no prior knowledge of a skill or knowledge is too big of a supposition. The movie scene is a good analogy to show the different prior skills of the learners. Despite the different skills and competencies with riding a bicycle, the whole Von Trapp group moves forward, including the advanced and the struggling riders and leaving no one behind.

Mr. David is a physical education teacher. In the 10th week of the semester, the course introduces a new sport—badminton. On the first day of the badminton class, Mr. David asks each student to show him the basic forehand and backhand moves of clear, smash, and drop. Why does Mr. David do that? He does that to find out the prior skills of the students to guide his instruction. Without knowing the prior skills, the physical education teacher would teach in the dark with inaccurate assumptions and ineffective instruction. Ineffective instruction means boring the advanced students and painfully dragging the struggling students.

The need to know the prior knowledge of the learner is manifested in an instructional technique known as K-W-L. The three-step technique was developed by Ogle (1986) and introduced successfully in the classroom. In using the technique, the teacher, like Mr. David, activates students' prior knowledge or skills by asking them what they already know or do not know. Then, based on what students already know, the teacher facilitates the students as a class or in small groups to set goals specifying what they want to learn. After the completion of the learning activities, students will discuss and draw conclusions about what they have learned. The K-W-L formula means what the learners Know (K), what the learners Want to know (W), and what the learners Learned (L).

A teacher has several reasons for using the K-W-L strategy in the classroom. For one, the it activates students' prior knowledge of the topic to be studied. Asking students what they already know invites students to think and connect to their prior experiences. Next, K-W-L gives a purpose to the unit of teaching by incorporating student input and giving them the ownership to learn. Finally, examining the information learned at the end of the class is a good way to compare what students want to know and to make an evaluation about the learning process. A K-W-L strategy is a tool that can be used effectively to guide instruction.

Have you seen small babies trying first to crawl and then to walk upright by balancing their bodies? Have you had the opportunity to watch older people using supports because they may feel insecure in their footing? How do you achieve a balance as you perform a variety of athletic activities such as running, jumping, and skipping? We have just raised critical questions regarding the concept of balance in progressive contexts in our lifespan. When we learn to balance, the prior skills of balancing will be revisited several times like a spiral, at a different level of complexity to achieve a deeper understanding of the movement concept. To physically balance our body through the years is continuous learning following a spiral path.

In a similar way, teaching is a spiral in the sense that the teacher needs to repeat and build on students' prior learning. Teachers who use spiral teaching continue to revisit and reinforce the concept throughout the school year and in successive years. The revisiting of the base concept is the activation and sustenance of prior knowledge with the addition of fresh meaning and competence.

Let us examine an English language arts (reading) strategy and a mathematics strategy to see how prior knowledge is effectively used in instruction.

In reading, the significance of prior knowledge such as vocabulary, main ideas, and literal expressions is underscored. It makes sense that the more a reader knows about the knowledge or skills, the better his or her reading comprehension will be. Thus, theoretically, students who have low basic reading skills but high background knowledge about a topic may be able to understand what the reading material intends to convey even if the words used are difficult. The combination of prior knowledge, which can be general to the text or specific to the subject matter, allows a reader to make inferences about meanings in a reading passage, and thus understand it.

Extensive reading is a key strategy in expanding the bank of background knowledge available to a reader. Through extensive reading of new words, meanings will be added to the knowledge bank of the reader. Teachers can help with this critical need to expand background knowledge by providing time for students to read and by supplying books that are interesting, grade-level appropriate, and varied in subject matter. Sustained Silent Reading (SSR) is a form of enrichment reading during which students read silently in a designated time period every day in school. An underlying assumption of SSR is that students learn and extend the skills of reading when given the opportunity to read more. There are different SSR forms under a variety of catchy names, such as Drop Everything and Read (DEAR) or Free Uninterrupted Reading (FUR).

In mathematics, the significance of prior knowledge arises in learning connections. Mathematics is often held distant by students because of its abstractness and inexplicit links to what students know about the real world. For that reason, the mathematics taught must be reasonable to the students and make sense with their prior knowledge to allow them to construct new meaning. An important factor in teaching for meaning is to connect the new ideas and skills to students' past knowledge and experience. For example, instruction in statistics can relate data collection and interpretation to public assessment polling of user satisfaction in a consumer report. It is recommended that teachers need to build on students' intuitive notions and methods about the subject matter in designing and delivering instruction. Please note that students in high-poverty schools may lack appropriate prior knowledge to make learning connections. This deficiency may be compensated through school enrichment activities supported by funding through the federal 21st Century Community Learning Centers program.

5.3. LEARNERS CONSTRUCT KNOWLEDGE

Every day, millions of students enter school wanting to learn, hoping to be stimulated, engaged, and treated well, and hoping to find meaning in what they do. And every day that we, educators, stimulate and challenge our students to focus their minds on meaningful tasks, to think about important issues, and to construct new understanding of their worlds, we—and they—achieve a meaningful victory.

—J. G. Brooks and M. G. Brooks (1999, 120)

Learners do not learn passively like tape recorders recording ideas in their memories. Learners construct cognitively in an attempt to understand how the world works. That students learn from real experience is a statement that has been studied and embraced for many years, prompting students to think, know, and do. This construction of knowledge is an educational tradition dating back to John Dewey (Dewey 1910/1991) and Jean Piaget (Piaget 1975/1985). Dewey proposed that learning should ideally organize around the interests of the learner, motivating him to actively deal with issues and solve problems. Piaget proposed that learning takes place when a learner's way of thinking leads to curiosity. This curiosity then leads to accommodation (cognitive change) to achieve a new level of cognitive equilibrium.

A person's knowledge is not a representation of the real world, but a collection of ideas that are adapted within the person's range of experience. In other words, the person's knowledge fits with the world, much like how a key fits into a lock. A learner constructs his own key by making sense of the world. Interestingly, many different keys can open a given lock, and this representation is only figurative and not real world. In teaching, it is strongly recommended that we employ many different instructional pathways leading to the final learning destination.

How do teachers develop a model of knowledge construction in teaching? Consider the following social science lesson. A high school teacher asks the students about how social policies in the 1980s affected the economic and educational achievement of the African American population in the United States. Instead of reading a section from the textbook, students can be coached to interpret census reports from the Internet and to generate their own hypotheses about social policies. Social science teachers often use other social science data such as demography and profiles of people to stimulate students for meaningful and real-world learning.

Read and compare the two science projects in figures 5.2 and 5.3. Consider the 10 questions below to understand the two constructivist lessons.

1. How is the learning experience posed around problems relevant to the real world?
2. What are the primary concepts developed through the learning experience?
3. How does the teacher support the students in a complex and open learning environment?
4. How does the teacher seek and value the students' point of view?
5. How is learning self-assessed by the student and finally assessed by the teacher?
6. How does the teacher challenge the students cognitively without giving them answers?
7. How can the teacher encourage collaborative group learning versus individual student learning?
8. How does the teacher help students to differentiate primary and secondary sources of information?
9. How will this lesson fit into the curriculum in alignment with the state learning standards?
10. How can this lesson be modified to accommodate the learning needs of different students?

The roles of a teacher in helping students to construct knowledge are often confusing. One might raise the question about how much a teacher should teach if

David John Foundation

572 Montego Drive
Bird, Illinois 60872
davidjohnfoundation@yahoo.com

October 29, 2011

Dear Dr. Ferguson,

The David John Foundation (DJF) is planning on building an All Sports Youth Camp in Birds, Illinois. This camp will include gymnastics, tennis, basketball, golf and water sports such as skiing, and sail-boating. Nevertheless, in the past year strange looking frog populations have been found. For your information, three recent pictures of strange looking frogs found in the area are attached. The strange appearance of frog ranges from missing limbs (left), eye (center) to extra limbs (right).

My concern as the chairman of DJF is that these strange looking frogs may be a sign that something is wrong. And if something is harming the frogs in the area, could this something also harm humans thus affecting the construction of the All Sports Youth Camp?

As the professor of the Environmental think tank, I would appreciate your helping me to collect, analyze, and form a persuasive argument for three supporting hypotheses regarding the reasons why frogs are strange looking in this area, and whether it is safe to build the All Sports Youth Camp in Birds, Illinois. I would like to present this argument at the December 1, 2011 board meeting to assist the foundation to decide the future of the Youth Camp construction proposal. Thank you so much for your help and expertise.

Sincerely,

David John

David John

Figure 5.2.   The David John Foundation Challenge
Source: Courtesy of the author.

students are to construct their own knowledge. The dilemma of a constructivist lesson is that too much or too little teaching will deter the students from actively learning. The roles of the teacher and the students evolve in a constructivist lesson—problem-based learning (figure 5.4). Starting from the left side of the diagram, and at the beginning of the lesson, the teacher engages students to reveal the

March 2, 2011

School of Education
Benedictine University
5700 College Road
Lisle, Illinois 60532-0900

Dear Dr. Wong,

Greetings from the U.S. Department of Energy. I am the new special project assistant to the Secretary of Energy and I am directed by Dr. Chu to ask your reputable geology research team to help us analyze and evaluate options in storing radioactive wastes. Under the new administration of President Obama, the Department of Energy is diligently looking for alternative radioactive waste disposal options. One site we use is the Yucca Mountain Repository in Nevada. This site is currently undergoing safety re-evaluation referencing the population of the region, the shipment of nuclear waste from its original source, the climate, and finally the geological structure and activities of the location.

Specifically, we ask that you advise the Department of Energy regarding whether nuclear waste should be stored at Yucca Mountain so we will present it at our next cabinet meeting on **Wednesday, May 5, 2011** for further discussion and decision. I thank you in anticipation for the help and the best to you and your students for the rest of the spring semester.

Yours sincerely,

Susan Glow

Susan Glow
Special Assistant to the Secretary of Energy
U.S. Department of Energy
Washington D.C.

Figure 5.3.   The Yucca Mountain Challenge
Source: Courtesy of the author.

rationale behind the learning. In the middle of the course, the teacher empowers students to explore and take charge of their own learning. Toward the end the students become independent learners, and the teacher remains a coach on the sidelines. A simple way to view the role relationship is that as one role increases, the other role decreases, and vice versa.

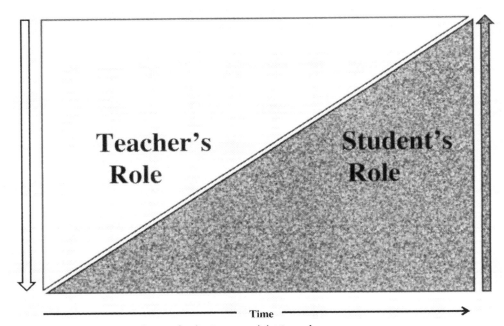

Figure 5.4.   Teacher-Student Roles in Constructivist Learning
Source: Courtesy of the author.

5.4. LEARNERS LEARN FROM MEANINGFUL EXPERIENCES

Tell me, and I will forget. Show me, and I may remember. Involve me and I will understand.

—Confucius

Erica adjusts her seat, the rearview mirrors, and the seat belt as her driver's education instructor looks on. *"Do you have a clear view of the road and the view around you? If not, please adjust your seat, the mirrors, and the belt again,"* urges the instructor. *"Check that the car transmission is in the park position before your turn the ignition key,"* continues the instructor. Erica goes through a typical behind-the-wheel lesson in driver's education to prepare for the state driver's license examination.

At the end of the driver's education lesson Erica leaves for her next class, health. The health lesson for the day is about learning an emergency lifesaving procedure called cardiopulmonary resuscitation, or CPR. The theory behind CPR is to keep the heart pumping and the oxygen flowing. *"How do you keep the heart pumping if the victim suffers a cardiac arrest and the heart stops pumping?"* asks the health teacher. After a few minutes of silence, the teacher continues, *"The rescuer has to perform artificial respiration for the victim until emergency care arrives."* The teacher then demonstrates on a CPR mannequin the technique of administering 30 chest compressions followed by two rescue breaths. Erica and the other students practice the CPR procedure as the health teacher supervises closely.

There are many ways to learn, and if the focus is to engage the learner in the process of what is being learned (e.g., learning how to drive and perform CPR), experiential

learning is a good model to follow. If instead the teaching focus is on direct information transfer (e.g., what is the structure and function of mitochondria of a cell), the best
way is probably to simply tell the student directly.

There are a number of truisms related to the purpose of experiential learning, and
the "*Tell me, and I will forget. Show me, and I may remember. Involve me and I will
understand*" statement by Confucius is probably a popular citation in teaching and
learning. John Dewey in his *Experience and Education* (1938) advocates for education to be based on the quality of the educational experience of the learner. For an
experience to be educational, Dewey believed that the criteria of continuity and interaction had to be met. *Continuity* means the sustained motivation of the person to stay
curious about learning. *Interaction* means the experience meeting the learning needs
of the person.

The modern foundation of pedagogy used in experiential learning is the learning
cycle prototype developed by Robert Karplus (1977). He basically developed the
learning process in a cycle of five phases: engagement, exploration, explanation,
elaboration, and evaluation.

In engagement, the teacher mentally engages students to whet their curiosity about
a problem, issue, or topic. Engagement is an invitation to learning. In exploration, the
teacher encourages the students to explore ideas and establish an experience base. In
explanation, the teacher seeks to reinforce understanding by soliciting explanations
from the students based on the established and prior knowledge. In elaboration, the
teacher challenges students to apply their conceptual understanding to different situations and to make purposeful connections and transitions. In evaluation, the teacher
encourages students to assess their learning; evaluation provides opportunities for
teachers to evaluate student achievement. The essence of the cycle is the experience
and the reflection of the learner; it is downright student-centered learning.

There are four major teaching issues stemming from the learning-cycle model. The
issues are: (1) the obscurity of students' prior knowledge with reference to students'
misconceptions; (2) the less-than-strategic placement of learning evaluation; (3) the
cyclic nature of the phases; and (4) the two-dimensionality of the cycle.

Where do we appropriately address students' misconceptions in the learning cycle?
A student may come to class with an established preconception of the topic. Unfortunately, some of the preconceptions are also misconceptions. These misconceptions, if
not clarified and corrected, will interfere with new learning.

When was the last time we heard students say that it is hot in the summer because
planet Earth is closer to the Sun at that time of the year? How do we proceed to teach
the four seasons if students are reluctant to give up their prior misconceived knowledge? When was the last time we heard students say that Abraham Lincoln's Eman-
cipation Proclamation of January 1863 freed all American slaves? The proclamation
applied only to the rebelling states not recognizing the power of the federal government. Most slaves were not immediately freed as a direct result of the proclamation.
It was only with the adoption of the Thirteenth Amendment in 1865 that slavery was
officially abolished throughout the United States.

The effective teacher will need to offer an alternative path to stimulate the student's
curiosity, to invite the student to question his prior knowledge, and to encourage him
to explore a better explanation for the issue at hand. Misconception should be elicited

for examination and clarification. In the learning cycle, an elicitation phase should follow closely after engagement.

The placement of evaluation in the learning cycle is at the very end. This is meant to be a summative evaluation, we assume. Nevertheless, this evaluation process can be strengthened by the addition of continuous formative assessments connecting to all phases of the cycle. A teacher in the process of engaging the students to learn found that students had marginal understanding of some prior knowledge. This formative assessment prompted the teacher to revisit an old concept and to put off the next phase of exploration for the time being. The adjustment of teaching strategies is guided continuously by the formative assessment of the teacher; this adjustment is otherwise known as fine-tuning. In this way, assessment informs instruction and permeates the phases of the cycle.

If the circular nature of the cycle is taken literally, then learning will keep going around and around, never reaching a learning destination. When learning is taken as a journey, which it is, then the circular path needs to be reconfigured to show a definite beginning and a definite finish. It is proposed that successful learning transfer can be designated the exit of the cycle. Interestingly, if the circular path is flat and continuous, it will be impossible to designate an exit. Hence the problematic two-dimensionality of the learning cycle is illogical.

Many teachers believe that the learning cycle is a form of scaffolding. The building of a physical scaffold depends on the careful layering of the structure. If the building knowledge or skills is likened to the building of a scaffold, then the learning cycle will no longer be flat or two-dimensional. Instead, the learning cycle will become a three-dimensional circular structure of a spiral going up. The building of a structure going up also implies an increase of potential energy as defined by the new higher position gained. Similarly, learning with a higher potential has a better chance of making connections to other areas of learning. The expression that teachers bring students to a new height of achievement may be offered to explain literally the three-dimensionality of learning.

In view of the four issues of the learning cycle discussed, a suggestion is made to improve the obscurity of handling student misconception; the placement of evaluation at the end of the cycle; the circular path of the learning cycle with no apparent exit; and the challenging interpretation of the two-dimensional cycle. A suggestion for improvement follows. First, an elicitation phase is added to the cycle; second, the evaluation process is made continuous; third, we designate learning transfer as the exit of the circle; and fourth, the cycle is reconfigured in a three-dimensional structure. All the suggestions for improvement point to the creation of a revised learning cycle, called a learning spiral, illustrated in figure 5.5 (Wong 2008).

Let us visit a high school science teacher to see how the different phases of the learning spiral are integrated. Ms. Smith teaches a lesson about the simple Mendelian genotype ratio of 1:2:1 for the offspring the first generation produced by crossing two purebred organisms. Ms. Smith uses a scenario based on personal interest and a societal issue of dog breeding. She shows photographs of two mixed-breed dogs. "*If the two dogs are the result of crossbreeding, then what can you expect about the characteristics of their parents?*" asks Ms. Smith. The teacher then shows four more dog pictures. "*If characteristics of the offspring resemble those of the parents, then*

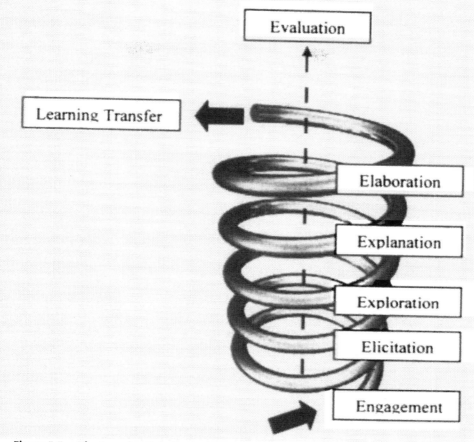

Figure 5.5. The Learning Spiral
Source: O. Wong (2008), "Revisiting the Learning Cycle and Its Implications for Science Instruction," SPECTRUM, volume 34, number 1.

who are the parents of the two dogs that I just showed?" asks Ms. Smith. The dog pictures prompt a number of questions regarding the possible offspring and parent characteristics. Toward the end of engagement students are stirred to find out more.

One student explains, *"The look of the offspring is the average of the two dog parents. If one parent has long hair and the other has short hair then the offspring will have the average of the parent, which will be medium-length hair."* This is obviously correct if a gene is expressed as incompletely dominant. Knowing that this is a misconception in the situation of a gene that expresses itself as completely dominant or recessive, Ms. Smith asks how it is possible for a tall offspring to have a tall parent and a short parent. At this point Ms. Smith draws out the misconception in elicitation. Often, when the ideas do not fit together, the teacher must help the learner to break down old misconceptions and reconstruct them.

Another student suggests that the different characteristic combinations in crossbreeding may be tested by using a physical model. A number of students agree to the model proposal due to their familiar experience (i.e., prior knowledge) with dice and board games. At this time, Ms. Smith introduces the game of chance through the use of four labeled ping-pong balls. Without looking, each student draws two balls at a time from a deep bowl. They then record the ball combination and record the results in a Punnett square displayed on the board. In this segment of learning, students are actively exploring to construct meaning.

With the collected data and the Punnett square, the students begin to realize and explain how the genes from each parent might combine to produce the offspring. In addition to showing the possible genotype of offspring, the Punnett square indicates how likely a particular offspring of this cross is to have a gene makeup. A Punnett square illustrates the results of a cross between to heterozygous individuals. The results are a 1:2:1 gene makeup ratio and a 3:1 appearance ratio.

The new knowledge/skill learned in the genetics lesson becomes familiar knowledge (i.e., monohybrid cross) on which to connect new learning (i.e., dihybrid cross); the spiral of learning reaches the ready state of learning transfer. Finally, evaluation of learning is continuous and allows the teacher to determine if the students have attained the understanding of concepts and knowledge. As teachers we need to remember that based in the cognitive learning principle of assimilation, the learning spiral implies that learning cannot be imposed on the learner. Instead it is developed progressively by the learner from conception and internalization.

People often talk about learning firsthand versus learning secondhand. Both kinds of learning involve experience of the learner. As teachers we know that any experience from firsthand learning (i.e., learning how to drive a car and perform CPR) will make a deeper impact on the learner than secondhand or simulated learning (i.e., doing the genetics activity using the Punnett square). In studying the teaching techniques of 2(HP) schools in chapter 2, we see that experiential learning is a dominant mode of teaching. In general, teachers make conscientious efforts to provide students with hands-on and minds-on experiences as time and resources permit.

Experiential learning is all fine, but what if the direct experience is not available, or what if the experience is time or cost prohibitive? These seem to be the fundamental challenges of experiential learning. More critically, one cannot perform a task endlessly just to get the essential learning out of it, when we inevitably make errors and fail along the way. Simulation learning may hold the answer.

Simulation is a form of experiential learning. Simulation learning may come in many different forms such as computer games, role-plays, or building models. But a true simulation experience has a specific goal in mind: to simulate or mimic a real system so that students can explore the problem and conceptualize the ideas to minimize the time and cost constraints.

"*Is simulation better then the real experience?*" is often a question raised. The answer to that question is an unequivocal "*yes and no.*" Hands-on learning experience with the real thing is always valuable. Unfortunately, that experience can be cost and time prohibitive. This is where simulation teaching comes in to help. Simulation teaching is instructional by design. Simulation proponents would say that simulation is better because it compresses time and removes extraneous details to concentrate on the main learning event. Unlike real life, simulations are designed to optimize learning.

Let us examine two simulated learning examples, one from the National Geographic Society and the other from ExploreLearning.

The National Geographic Society (NGS) is a good partner in education. NGS has publications and websites that deliver high-quality educational information. An interactive simulation website (www.nationalgeographic.com/forcesofnature/interactive/index.html?section=v) investigates the forces of nature, including tornadoes, hurricanes, volcanoes, and earthquakes. To study the forces in nature from direct experience is life threatening. Thanks to computer simulation, students can simulate an earthquake scenario by manipulating the variables such as the amount of force and the characteristics of the ground. The National Geographic Society is one of the largest nonprofit scientific and educational institutions in the world. The institution offers many quality educational programs for children and adults, and some of the programs are free of charge.

Would it not be nice if students could relive the legendary experience of Galileo more than 400 years ago from the top of the Leaning Tower of Pisa to study the behavior of free-falling objects? Unfortunately, there is no rewind button and there is no turning back of time. To relive the experience, students have to work on some simulated experience. Figure 5.6 is a representation of the scenario (www.explorelearning .com/index.cfm?method=cResource.dspView&ResourceID=650) where students can select and drop objects from the top of the tower and record the speed of the fall. In the true spirit of learning, this simulation can be performed using a wide selection of variables relating to the falling objects and the experiment's conditions. Explorelearning is the company behind this simulation program. It is different from National Geographic's program in that it is subscription based and not free.

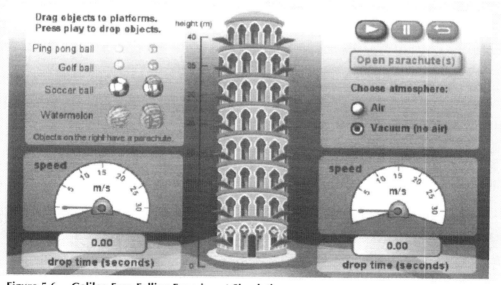

Figure 5.6. Galileo Free-Falling Experiment Simulation
Source: Used with permission from ExploreLearning. www.explorelearning.com/index.cfm?method=cResource.ds|View&
ResourceID=650

5.5. LEARNERS LEARN FROM
APPROPRIATE SOCIAL INTERACTION

An essential instructional skill that all teachers need is to know how and when to structure students' learning goals competitively, individualistically, and cooperatively. Each goal structure has its place; an effective teacher will use all three appropriately.

—David and Roger Johnson (1994)

"*Break into groups of two now that you have finished reading* Beowulf, *the old English heroic epic poem*," says the teacher. "*What are we supposed to do in the small group?*" ask several eager students almost at the same time without raising their hands. "*Thank you for asking. In your small group, please discuss the different antagonist roles of Grendel, Grendel's mother, and the unnamed dragon against Beowulf, the protagonist. You have 20 minutes for the discussion, and we will reconvene after that to share your discussion,*" answers the teacher.

In this teaching scenario, the teacher poses an open-ended academic question and gives students time to think and discuss. The thinking part of the activity is crucial because it gives students a chance to start formulating and retrieving information from the reading assignment. Students then pair with another student and discuss their ideas about the protagonist-antagonist question. The small-group structure gives all students the opportunity to share their ideas. This is also important because students are given the opportunity to construct and discuss their knowledge to find out what they do and do not know.

Various names are given to teaching strategies involving social interaction, including think-pair-share, cooperative learning, collaborative learning, interactive learning, jigsaw learning, round robin brainstorming, team pair solo, three-minute review, and study team.

A cooperative learning group of two, or think-pair-share, is the smallest grouping in social interactive learning. Think-pair-share was first proposed by Lyman (1981). The strategy is relatively low risk because the small group size tightens the accountability and minimizes off-task activities. It is ideal for teachers who are new to collaborative learning and may be apprehensive about classroom management. After the small-group discussion, the instructor solicits student comments. Students are much more willing to respond after they have had a chance to discuss their ideas with a classmate because even if the answer is wrong, the embarrassment is shared. In addition, the responses received are often more intellectually concise because students have already had a chance to reflect on their own ideas.

The social interaction strategies are widely used across other disciplines. Let us now study the use of the social interactive strategies in mathematics. Recent results from Trends in the International Mathematics and Science Study (TIMSS) video show that Japanese teachers structure instruction around carefully chosen problems, allowing students to interact when solving these problems. Later, teachers also provide opportunities to share their solution methods in a whole-class discussion; this results in increased math-problem-solving achievement. More important, these gains come with no achievement loss on standardized achievement tests. It is shown that when students receive opportunities to develop and share their own solution methods, they are better able to apply mathematical knowledge in solving new problems.

From the English language arts and mathematics lessons described, one can identify five basic elements of the social interactive teaching strategy: (1) assign groups (regardless of size), (2) provide guidelines, (3) assign tasks, (4) assess, and (5) share results. There are general guiding principles for interactive learning groups. The first one is to create group tasks that require interdependence. The students in a group must perceive that they sink or swim together and unless the group succeeds, the individual does not succeed. Knowing that peers rely on one another is a powerful motivator for group work. The second principle is that the work must be relevant. Students must perceive the group tasks as integral to the course objectives and not just busywork.

The theory of social interaction learning goes back to Lev Vygotsky (1978), when the Russian psychologist asserted that social interaction plays a critical role in critical cognitive development. Vygotsky felt that social learning precedes development. In essence, he said that basic functions in the child's cultural development occur two times: first, on the social level, and later on the individual level. Simply put, learning takes place first between people, and then inside the person.

5.6. LEARNERS LEARN FROM REGULAR PRACTICE AND FEEDBACK

Development of basic knowledge and skills to the necessary levels of automatic and errorless performance requires a great deal of drill and practice . . . drill and practice activities should not be slighted as low level. Carried out properly, they appear to be just as essential to complex and creative intellectual performance as they are to the performance of a virtuoso violinist.

—Jerome Brophy (1986)

A husband and a wife talk to their fifth-grade son, Gordon, and fourth-grade daughter, Terri, about their impression of their math teachers. As Gordon and Terri compare notes on their experiences, the parents ask about their math teacher Mr. Johnson. The parents cannot believe the homework load that Mr. Johnson sends home each night with unbelievable drill-and-practice worksheets. Both Gordon and Terri love Mr. Johnson. They do not love the worksheets, but they really like how the worksheets drill the materials into their brains. "*Mr. Johnson is a great teacher,*" both children exclaim. Terri says that she and her friends look forward to having Mr. Johnson again the next year. "*It is drill to understand. It is not drill to kill!*" Gordon adds.

Drill and practice is a mythical teaching strategy that has become a bad word in education. The strategy is quite the opposite of the constructivist learning discussed earlier. Drill and practice produces busywork and rote memorization, and diminishes creativity, some say. Therefore, for a teacher to spend a long time on repetitive tasks is a sign that learning is not creative. On the other hand, the acquisition of knowledge or skills such as the memorization of spelling words and the practicing of arithmetic facts such as the multiplication table are the foundations and reinforcement.

The human brain is the main organ of learning. It is biologically *not* a muscle and should not be thought of as such. However, analogously the brain can be thought of as a muscle because simply telling students that the brain is like a muscle leads to better learning. Of course, it's still controversial, and it's *not* about the brain's being biologically similar to muscle. It's about *thinking* about brain development as being like muscle development. Drill and practice matter in learning because they build better meaning and longer duration in learning.

In mathematics, "number sense" is an important construct relating to having an intuitive feel for number size and number combination. Number sense is a national and state learning standard. It includes computing, estimating, sensing number magnitudes, moving between representation systems of numbers, and judging reasonableness of numerical results. In the classroom, it is an important student-learning outcome and a foundation for building higher mathematical skills. Drill and practice is a very common strategy for teaching number sense. It comes in a paper-based format (i.e., worksheets and game cards) as well as a computer based format (i.e., computer activities). Many schools including 2(HP) schools studied are shifting from paper to technology-based strategies for drill and practice. Students tend to enjoy the computer activities more than the paper activities. "I learn and I have fun" is what helps to demystify the "bad boy" of education.

The Kumon Math enrichment method is embraced by millions of schoolchildren in Korea, Japan, and Singapore, countries that score the highest on worldwide mathematics achievement tests. Kumon Math emphasizes calculations, which the National Council of Teachers of Mathematics (NCTM) has recognized to be a weak area of American teaching (Hoff 2000). Kumon seeks to make computational skills automatic by practice, claiming that repetition is a significant factor in improving student achievement. Benjamin Bloom advanced the concept of mastery learning. He explained that three elements—sufficient time, appropriate instruction, and corrective feedback—will enable 95% of students to learn what only 20% were thought to be capable of (Bloom 1968). Kumon uses all three elements.

One important strategy that is popularly used or modified in the classroom is the Madeline Hunter's model of teaching. The model has several steps:

1. Lesson Objective—The teacher has a clear idea of what to teach regarding what the student should be able to know and do. The teacher can use Bloom's Taxonomy of Educational Objectives to determine the level of teaching complexity.
2. Standards—The teacher needs to know and share with students the standards of performance to be expected. This can be an explanation of the lesson type or procedures to be followed.
3. Anticipatory Set—This is the invitation to learn. It is similar to Ausubel's advance organizer (Ausubel 1960) and the engagement phase of the learning spiral. The purpose of the set is to put students in a receptive frame of mind and to grab their attention.
4. Teaching: Input—The teacher provides the needed information for students to gain knowledge or skills. This is normally a large-group presentation.

5. Teaching: Modeling—The teacher shows examples to reinforce the presented knowledge or skill. Here the students are taken to the application level of learning.
6. Teaching: Checking for Understanding—The teacher determines whether students have "gotten it" before proceeding. If there is any doubt that the students have not understood, the concept/skill should be retaught before practice begins.
7. Guided Practice—The teacher demonstrates how certain knowledge is conceptualized or how a certain skill is implemented. This is similar to having the teacher say, "This is how I do it, now let us see how you do it after me."
8. Independent Practice—The teacher provides an opportunity for each student to demonstrate the grasp of new learning. This learning opportunity in the form of class work or homework is provided on a repeated schedule so that learning is not forgotten. The learning exercise provides different contexts for real-world learning. The teacher moves around the class to determine the level of mastery and to provide individual remediation as needed.
9. Closure—The teacher brings the lesson to an appropriate conclusion and asks students to bring thoughts together in their own minds, to make sense out of what has just been taught. Closure is the activity of reviewing and clarifying key learning points from the lesson and securing them in the student's conceptual network.

The implementation of the Hunter's model of teaching may vary in the specific sequence of steps. However, in essence, it is a combination of teacher input (i.e., teaching) and student output (i.e., learning). What is important in the Hunter's model of teaching strategy is the illustration of student practice in a combination of guided and independent activities to eventually secure learning.

Educational research spanning decades indicates that effective instruction demands the orchestration of a wide spectrum of strategies that must be adapted to specific learning contexts. This chapter reviews various research-proven strategies grounded in supporting the learning environment, understanding the prior knowledge of students, giving students the opportunity to construct knowledge, giving students the opportunity to connect learning with meaningful experience, permitting students to learn through appropriate social interactions, and the opportunity to practice what has been learned. It is important to note that any attempt to improve student achievement as seen in the 2(HP) school study is driven by the consistent execution of effective instructional strategies by the instructional staff.

REFERENCES

Ausubel, D. P. 1960. The use of advance organizer in the learning and retention of meaningful verbal material. *Journal of Educational Psychology* 51:267–72.
Bloom, B. 1968. Mastery learning. In *Mastery learning: Theory and practice*, ed. J. Block, 47–63. New York: Holt & Winston.
Brooks, J. G., and M. G. Brooks. 1999. *In search of understanding: The case for constructive classrooms*. 2nd ed. Alexandria, VA: Association for Supervision and Curriculum Development.
Brophy, J. 1986. Teacher influences on student achievement. *American Psychologist* 41:1069–77.

Dewey, J. 1938. *Experience and education*. New York: Macmillan.

———. 1991. *How we think*. Buffalo, NY: Prometheus Books. (Orig. pub. 1910.)

Edmonds, R. 1977. *Search for effective schools: The identification of city schools that are instructionally effective for poor children. Washington, DC: U.S. Department of Education.*

Hoff, D. J. 2000. Math revisions add emphasis on basic skills. *Education Week*, April 19, at www.edweek.org/ew/ewstory.cfm?slug=32nctm.h19.

Johnson, D., and R. Johnson. 1994. *Learning together and alone: Cooperative, competitive, and individualistic learning*. Boston: Allyn & Bacon.

Karplus, R., et al. 1977. *Teaching and the development of reasoning*. Berkeley: University of California Press.

Kolb, D. A. 1984. *Experiential learning*. Englewood Cliffs, NJ: Prentice Hall.

Lyman, F. 1981. The responsive classroom discussion. In *Mainstreaming digest*, ed. A. S. Anderson. College Park: University of Maryland College of Education.

Ogle, D. M. 1986. K-W-L: A teaching model that develops active reading of expository text. *Reading Teacher* 39:564–70.

Piaget, J. 1985. *The equilibrium of cognitive structure*. Trans. T. Brown and K. J. Thanpys. Chicago: University of Chicago Press. (Orig. pub. 1975.)

Vygotsky, L. S. 1978. *Mind and society: The development of higher mental processes*. Cambridge, MA: Harvard University Press.

Wong, H. 2001. *The first days of school: How to be an effective teacher*. Harry K. Wong Publications, Inc. www.effectiveteaching.com.

Wong, O. 2008. Revisiting the learning cycle and its implication to science instruction. *Spectrum* 34 (1): 26–32.

Chapter Six

The 2(HP) Assessment

Teacher Sally has just finished an introductory unit on the addition of fractions. Students were participatory and paying attention. Everything seems to be going well, and students seem to "get it." However, do they? Let us look at the following teacher-student exchanges.

"You have learned that the sum of 3 + 5 is 8," says teacher Sally. *"Yeah, yeah, yeah,"* chant the students. Writing $3 + 5 = 8$ on the board, the teacher continues, *"What if I write the same numbers in a fraction . . . ?"* The teacher writes 3/5 on the board. *"Now please tell me the sum of 3/5 and 3/5."* Three students raise their hands immediately. *"What is the answer? Please explain the answer. Jim, you go first. Jan, and Erica you can follow Jim,"* the teacher continues. *"The sum of 3/5 and 3/5 is 6/10 because the sum of the numerators is 6, and the sum of the denominator is 10,"* says Jim confidently. *"The sum of 3/5 and 3/5 is 6/5, because you add the numerators and you just do not need to add the denominator; they are the same,"* says Jan. *"The answer is 1 and 1/5, because the sum of 3/5 and 3/5 is 6/5, and 6/5 can be simplified as 1 and 1/5,"* says Erica impatiently.

Teacher Sally's perception that students "get it" seems to be quite different from the students' answers. If Jim, Jan, and Erica are a student sample of the class, then only two-thirds of the class truly understands the operation of adding fractions. It is a common mistake that teachers generally conclude that students have learned and are ready to move on to the next unit of the curriculum. From the sample student responses, Jim has the concept all wrong; Jan has the right answer, and Erica has the right answer plus an extended understanding of converting an improper fraction to a mixed number.

The above scenario raises an additional question: How likely is it that teacher Sally knew that Jim had a misconception about fraction addition? The answer is that she probably did not realize that Jim (and maybe several other students in the class) did not know the fraction addition operation after she finished teaching the topic. This leads to the central role of assessment in teaching and high-stakes testing as facts of teaching life.

6.1. AN EVOLUTIONARY HISTORY OF EDUCATIONAL REFORMS

America is currently undergoing a controversial bout of education reform, and the assessment of students and teachers is right at the center of the reform movement. The beginning of the current education reform goes back almost 30 years.

In 1983, the quality of American education was reported in *A Nation at Risk*. The report described the problems afflicting American education. This document famously stated:

> Our Nation is at risk. Our once unchallenged preeminence in commerce, industry, science, and technological innovation is being overtaken by competitors throughout the world. This report is concerned with only one of the many causes and dimensions of the problem, but it is the one that undergirds American prosperity, security, and civility. We report to the American people that while we can take justifiable pride in what our schools and colleges have historically accomplished and contributed to the United States and the well-being of its people, the educational foundations of our society are presently being eroded by a rising tide of mediocrity that threatens our very future as a Nation and a people. What was unimaginable a generation ago has begun to occur—others are matching and surpassing our educational attainments.

In 1989, President George H. W. Bush and the nation's governors held a national education conference to establish six broad goals to address the issues raised in *A Nation at Risk*. The conference report emphasized the need to develop student performance standards.

In 1994, the Goals 2000: Educate America Act was established. It set educational goals by providing a national reform framework to improve student achievement. The framework includes such ambitious goals as to increase the high school graduation rate to 90%; to make American students first in the world in mathematics and science achievement; to ensure that every school will a disciplined environment conducive to learning with no drugs, violence, or unauthorized presence of firearms and alcohol; and the list goes on.

In 1996, the National Education Summit was held with the governors of more than 40 states and national business leaders; it aimed to set up clear subject matter content standards at the state and local levels.

In 2001, the No Child Left Behind Act (NCLB) made it a law that all students and schools are accountable for new and rigorous assessment standards. Prior to NCLB, the measures of success had not been focused heavily on student achievement. With NCLB, school success is measured heavily by whether or not students learn.

In the past decades, we have witnessed the rigorous shaping of American education. The thread that runs through each of the reform efforts is that each state of the union has established standards and assessments to measure students' attainment of those standards. History shows that each era of education reform has escalated accountability, with more assessment aimed at higher student achievement and more effective schools. One trend is clear as we follow the shaping of American education reform through time (figure 6.1). There is an increasing demand for accountability (i.e., assessment) and academic success for all students (Wong and Lam 2007).

Education Reform Movement (1983 – 2001)

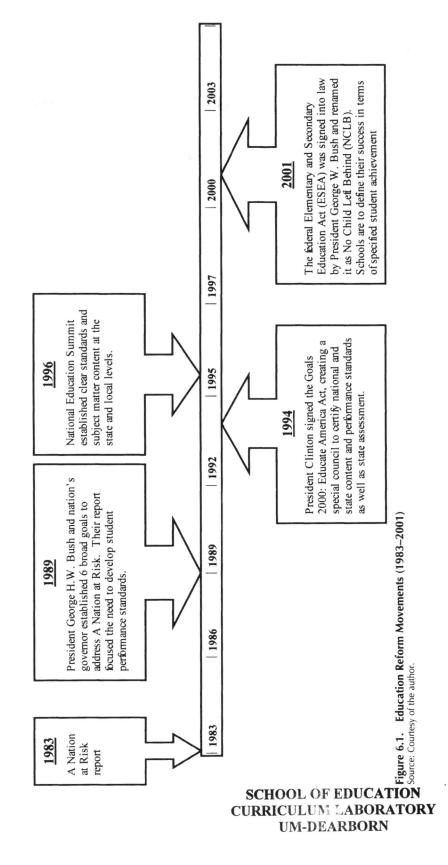

1983

A Nation at Risk report

1989

President George H.W. Bush and nation's governor established 6 broad goals to address A Nation at Risk. Their report focused the need to develop student performance standards.

1996

National Education Summit established clear standards and subject matter content at the state and local levels.

1994

President Clinton signed the Goals 2000: Educate America Act, creating a special council to certify national and state content and performance standards as well as state assessment.

2001

The federal Elementary and Secondary Education Act (ESEA) was signed into law by President George W. Bush and renamed it as No Child Left Behind (NCLB). Schools are to define their success in terms of specified student achievement

| 1983 | 1986 | 1989 | 1992 | 1995 | 1997 | 2000 | 2003 |

Figure 6.1.   Education Reform Movements (1983–2001)
Source: Courtesy of the author.

6.2. ASSESSMENT OF STUDENT LEARNING—WHY?

In the attempt to answer the why question, there is a need to revisit teacher Sally's lesson. The success of her lesson on the addition of fractions depends on the students' understanding of the fraction operation concept. If Sally did not make an assessment and moved on to the next unit of instruction, Jim and probably more students would hold a misconception about the topic. Failure breeds failure, and the problem would compound for additional future failures if left unattended and uncorrected.

The assessment of student learning is the duty of every teacher. It is no surprise, then, that a typical teacher can spend a significant amount of time engaging the students in some type of assessment activities. Unfortunately, this is one task that many teachers do not enjoy doing and do not do well. Assessment should be used to reinforce, rather than work against, the role of being a teacher.

Teachers use assessment to collect information about how much knowledge and and how many skills students have learned, and to determine what level of learning is acceptable. In the first part of assessment, for example, the teacher may measure the students' level of mathematical reasoning by counting the number of problems correctly solved. The activity just described is called *measurement*. In a classroom, the number will be compared to an established rule system to create a ranking such as a letter grade to reflect how much of the mathematical reasoning ability different students have. The judging activity described is called *evaluation*. In a broad sense, assessment broadly involves measurement and evaluation.

Teachers have a number of methods to assess what students have learned. The methods selected depend on the purpose of the assessment. Is the assessment for knowing about something (i.e., knowledge), or for knowing how to do something (i.e., skills)? Is the assessment going to be a nongraded activity (informal), or a graded activity (formal)? Figure 6.2 describes a wide variety of assessment methods; some uses are narrow (i.e., performance assessment), and some are broad based (i.e., written test). Figure 6.2 shows that the selection of methods on the right is driven by the purpose of assessment on the left. All the methods of assessment will eventually converge to make a value judgment called *evaluation*. In this sense, assessment is formative and continuous while evaluation is summative and final in nature. A description of the specific methods will be discussed in the rest of this chapter.

Using the student assessment data, the teacher can decide what to adjust in teaching. Reteaching is one method of revisiting a topic that students fail to grasp. Reteaching does not mean doing more of the same. If a strategy does not work the first time, how can the same be effective the second time, or even the third time around? In the 2(HP) schools, many teachers are able to deploy different teaching methods when students encounter difficulties in understanding knowledge or skills. Under the current NCLB accountability system, teachers aim to achieve 100% student proficiency in mathematics and reading, and to reteach a topic for better understanding remains a challenge for many.

6.3. ASSESSMENT OF STUDENT ATTENDANCE

Many teachers normally think of assessment as just a test of students' academic knowledge and skills. How often do teachers think of student attendance assessment

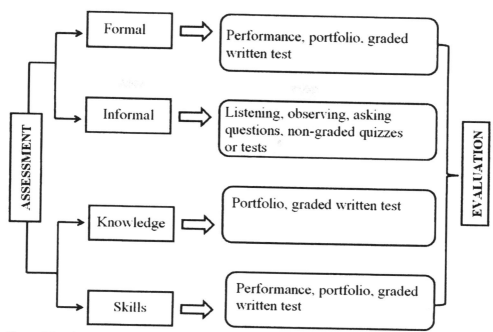

Figure 6.2. Assessment Methods
Source: Courtesy of the author.

as something that is as important, if not more important than assessing mathematics or reading? Assessment of student attendance is not only important but a legal require-ment of schools. The assessment of student attendance, and addressing the problem should it arise, is seen as a top priority for all the 2(HP) schools.

Student attendance and student learning are the two basics of every school day for the simple reason that students need to come to school to learn. Poor attendance alerts the school that the student is disengaging from the school process. It may fur-ther reflect a lack of student motivation and/or inadequate home support. All in all, the school attendance problem can be related to the community, home, school, and classroom (i.e., students and teachers). There are attendance factors (i.e., community and family) that we have little or no control over. There are other factors (i.e., school and classroom) that school can change. It is only obvious that teachers would prefer to invest more time and resources in factors that they believe will make a difference to improve student attendance.

Community variables contributing to poor school attendance are complex because they deal with the culture of a complex organization such as an inner-city school com-munity. The challenges can very much be inadequate school community support with high incidences of criminal activities. Family-related variables to poor attendance are many. They could be high family mobility, low family income, non-English-speaking family, and dysfunctional home. It all boils down to the family's setting low expec-tations for students to attend school. Many of the 2(HP) schools are plagued with problems that we just described. Miraculously, these schools overcome the odds and student achievement prevails. This is why 2(HP) schools are unique and envied by other schools.

Truancy is unexcused and excessive absence. It is one of the top problems of schools in big cities, negatively impacting academic performance. A major prevention and intervention strategy of truancy is the firm establishment and implementation of an attendance policy based on the compulsory school attendance mandate. 2(HP) school staff members are familiar with the attendance policy and they respond and enforce it swiftly in lieu of making other personal decisions.

As part of the assessment system, schools can systematically track student attendance, test scores, grades, behavior referrals, and family participation in school records. The assessment of these records can help to identify students most at risk for truancy and thus refer them for swift prevention efforts. Prevention efforts might include supports to improve attendance, programs to encourage parent involvement, early intervention for academic challenges, and partnerships with community business to better connect school to work.

How can teachers help to improve school attendance? They can be the role models and the enablers for students. Instead of getting a narrow view of why the student is not successful, have the student identify achievable goals from the school experience. Teachers can encourage the student to attend school regularly and sponsor extracurricular activities such as athletics programs or clubs.

One other strategy that the teacher can use to encourage school attendance is to give students a taste of school success. Students tend to repeat the same behavior of coming to school to achieve the same successful experience. For that reason, teachers need to reflect and assess their own behaviors to see if what they do is helping students to be successful. Teachers can reflect on such questions as: (1) Am I being fair and consistent to students? (2) Is the class environment conducive to learning? (3) Is my teaching engaging? (4) Do I address learning problems and give students the appropriate help and intervention? (5) Do I build students' self-confidence by appropriate student recognition?

High-performing students begin with good school attendance. This is why the No Child Left Behind law requires schools to attain a high percentage of student attendance and graduation (for high school only). Figure 6.3 highlights the variables of student attendance discussed. 2(HP) educators set a high priority on student attendance to pave the road to student success.

6.4. ASSESSMENT OF STUDENT LEARNING—INFORMAL

Teachers use a broad spectrum of assessment methods, and some are informal. Informal assessment can be as simple as observing, listening, and asking questions beyond just giving tests or quizzes. Teachers make informal student assessments all the time, and these assessments are an indispensable tool for decision making. For example, after seeing a few students making the same kind of mistakes in reading comprehension, the teacher might decide to give extra help to the students making the mistakes so other students may reshape their thinking. Informal assessments can be perceived as simple and frequent checks to monitor teaching and learning.

School administrators do informal assessment all the time. They walk the halls and they make in-and-out classroom visits. The informal walk-throughs and visits can be broken down into three areas: the learning environment, the curriculum, and the instruction.

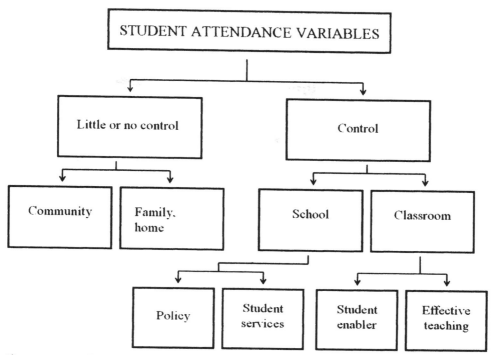

Figure 6.3. Student Attendance Variables
Source: O. Wong and Ming-Long Lam. (2007). *Using Data Analysis to Improve Student Learning: Toward 100% Proficiency*. Lanham, MD: Rowman & Littlefield Education.

The person walking through may look at the facilities to make sure that they are safe and orderly. Are students wandering the hallway instead of attending classes? Is the hallway clean and orderly? The person may also look at the walls and bulletin board for instructional artifacts such as student work, paintings, charts, and so on. An informal assessment of the learning environment is to check whether students are time-on-task, an important indicator of engagement of student learning.

Walking through to assess the alignment of the instruction to the state standards and the school curriculum is crucial. The person will assess the content, context, and cognitive level of the teaching activities. Whether or not the taught curriculum aligns with the state learning standards is a recurring question the administrator asks during the walk-through observation.

Last, the walk-through administrator will focus on two broad areas of instruction. The first one is general teaching practices. This broad area may include such strategies as comparing, contrasting, student summarizing and taking notes, reinforcing efforts and giving praise, practice and feedback, use of nonlinguistic representations, cooperative learning, generating and testing hypotheses, cues, questioning, strategies, use of advance organizers, active participation, meaningful teacher-student interaction, classroom management, and the list goes on. The second area is specific to a school. It is usually a focus area (e.g., literacy) of improvement from the current school improvement plan.

6.5. ASSESSMENT OF STUDENT LEARNING—FORMAL

In contrast to informal assessments, assessments designed to collect student information systematically for judgment purposes are formal. Teachers commonly use three types of formal assessments: performance assessments; portfolio assessments; and written, or paper-and-pencil, assessments.

When a student writes an essay, builds a science diorama, paints a picture, takes a photograph, runs a track, sings a song, plays a musical instrument, or does a project presentation and the teacher grades him, the teacher is using the performance assessment method. The teacher is interested in finding out the student's ability to do something. The assessment is based on the student's performing a task to demonstrate his ability to do it. For all practical purposes, a paper-and-pencil test will not be able to honestly assess the ability of a student in physical education, fine arts, or writing.

Performance assessment tends to be subjective if a teacher does not use an assessment rubric. If a person is the parent of an elementary or middle school child, he or she may have heard the word *rubric* and wondered what it meant. A rubric is a scoring tool that lists the judging criteria for a piece of work such as an essay. An assessment rubric helps students and teachers to define the quality of work.

Let us examine an example of a writing assessment rubric. Writing is a collection of complex skills that involve the use of voice, word choice, content ideas, organization, sentence fluency, and conventions. How can the teacher determine that one paper is weak and another is a wow? An analysis of a six-point writing rubric (figure 6.4) on writing conventions will help both the student and the teacher to reference the "standard" and understand the quality of the performance.

Portfolio assessment is the second type of formal assessment commonly used by teachers. A portfolio is similar to a file folder collecting sample work artifacts such as essays, projects, reports, and videotaped performances. Teachers and students can analyze the artifacts (with the help of a rubric again!) to determine learning growth in an area. For example, a student with a writing portfolio can compare his writing at the beginning, middle, and end of the school year to verify his growth in writing skills. With the advance of technology, a portfolio can be electronic, or computerized. Electronic portfolios are becoming increasingly popular because of their quick and easy access to a large volume of storage space.

Paper-and-pencil assessment is the third type. It is the most frequently used assessment in the classroom and in many high-stakes standardized state examinations and college admission tests. The format of the assessment may include fill-in-the-blanks, true-or-false questions, matching, and the ever-popular multiple-choice test. Unlike performance assessments and portfolio assessments, the multiple-choice, also called forced-choice or selected-response, examination is classified as an objective measure simply because the scorer (this can be a scoring machine) does not make a decision about the quality of an answer. The scoring objective of a multiple-choice examination is to find out whether the answer is correct or not correct, period.

Let us study and compare the grade 4 reading tests of Oregon and Washington states (figures 6.5 and 6.6). The design of the two state tests is similar in that the test

Level	Description
1 (Not yet)	Numerous errors in usage, spelling, capitalization, and punctuation. The text is difficult to read. The writing is characterized by the omission of or incorrect basic punctuation; frequent spelling errors; paragraph breaks are irregular and bear no relation to the text organization; capitalization is random.
2 (Emerging)	The writing shows little control of standard writing conventions. Frequent errors impede reading. The writing is characterized by little control over basic conventions; many end-of-sentence punctuation errors; misspelling of common words; paragraphs that run together; capitalization is inconsistent; grammatical errors impede reading.
3 (Developing)	The writing shows some control of standard writing conventions. The writing is characterized by some control over basic conventions and the text may be too simple to show mastery; correct end-of-sentence punctuation with internal punctuation errors; spelling errors distracts reading; paragraphs sometimes run together; some capitalization errors; grammatical errors do not block meaning but distract the reader.
4 (Competent)	The writing shows control of standard writing conventions. The writing is characterized by control over convention used although a wide range is not demonstrated; correct end-of-sentence punctuation with some incorrect internal punctuation; spellings are usually correct; good paragraph breaks to reinforce the organizational structure; minor capitalization mistakes; occasional lapses in correct grammar usage.
5 (Experienced)	The writing shows strong control of standard writing conventions. The writing is characterized by very good control of conventions; effective use of punctuation; correct spelling; appropriate paragraph breaks to reinforce organizational structure; correct capitalization; correct grammar contributing to clarity and style; use of a wide range of conventions.
6 (Wow!)	The writing shows exceptional strong control of standard writing conventions. The writing is characterized by strong control of conventions to show styles; strong punctuation use to guide the reader; correct spelling even of difficult words; excellent paragraph breaks; correct capitalization; correct grammar usage; use of a wide range of conventions in long and complex sentence structures.

Figure 6.4. Writing Assessment Rubric—Conventions
Source: Courtesy of the author.

taker will first read a passage and then answer questions. It is obvious that the assessment objective of the two state test examples is reading comprehension. Compare further the question asked in both tests. One Oregon test question asks for the author's purpose, and the Washington test question asks for the author's message. In both, the commonality is the author's idea(s) of writing, or the author's point of view.

WISHBONE'S WISH

In this passage, author Michael Jan Friedman introduces us to Wishbone and some of his friends. In this part of the story, Wishbone watches as his friends play a game called roller hockey.

THERE WAS ONLY ONE PROBLEM. Wishbone wasn't a roller-blading kind of guy. Feet were more his kind of thing — four of 'em, to be exact. So all he could do was watch. The kids blasted back and forth across the gym floor, warming up for their chance at roller hockey glory.

Sighing, Wishbone snuffled and rested his head on his front paws. He wanted to be in the middle of the action. Center stage, as it were. That was where he really came alive.

If he couldn't take part in the game, he could still root for his favorite humans. Joe, Samantha, and David were zipping around the place in their helmets and gloves and pads. They flipped a red ball back and forth with considerable grace and accuracy.

Joe was the friendly, <u>easygoing</u> kid Wishbone lived with. He was also the best, most loyal friend anyone could ask for. David was the inventor in the group. He was always ready to roll up his sleeves and build an answer to any problem.

And Samantha? She was the kind of human a person just couldn't help liking — whether that person had two legs

Figure 6.5.   Oregon State Reading Test
Source: Reading sample test (grade 4). Printed with permission from the Oregon Department of Education.

It is interesting that if we are to map the reading test item backward, we can clearly find an author's point of view in reading comprehension under the state reading standard! It is even more interesting that regardless of the state, one can find this in all the state reading standards across the nation. One important lesson learned from this analysis is that the teacher needs to drive the instruction based on the state standards if he or she is to prepare the students well for the mandatory state examination. After all, who can argue against the importance of an author's purpose in literacy and reading comprehension?

Trail Mix
by Susie Post-Rust

1   Lester Erhart's dogs are jumping and yelping, ready to go. Standing behind Colt, Ben, Cid, and Blazer on a sled, Lester adjusts his face mask so only his eyes show. The 13-year-old's misty breath escapes as he waits in the 15-below-zero cold.

2   "Five. Four. Three. Two. One. *Go!*" the announcer calls.

3   "All right!" Lester yells.

4   The team takes off with a jerk. "It's like you're floating on air," Lester says. He hears the wind rustling his jacket and the dogs' paws beating the snowy path. And, of course, the barking.

Kathleen Blevins, 15, heads for the finish line in the six-dog race.

5   This is the 2001 Junior North American/International Federation of Sled Dog Sports Junior World Championships in Fairbanks, Alaska. Kids and sled dogs race down a snowpacked trail through the woods. There's only one musher per sled, but make no mistake: this is a team sport.

Mush Pit

6   It's a tight friendship between dog and musher. Who else is a musher going to depend on if his sled tips over five miles into a lonely trail? The dogs—Alaskan huskies and hounds—depend on the mushers for daily feeding, cleaning, training, and love.

7   But no amount of bonding prepared Britni Browning, 13, for what happened to her. The best of her four dogs sat down in the middle of the race—*four* times!

8   "I knew I wasn't going to win," Britni says. "But I got off the sled, petted Whitey, and told him he was doing well. If he thought I was mad, he'd never get up!"

Figure 6.6. Washington State Reading Test
Source: Used with permission from the Office of Superintendent of Public Instruction (State of Washington).

Let us study and compare the grade 4 mathematics state tests of Oregon and Washington (figure 6.7) next. The design of the two state tests is similar in that the test taker will first interpret a graph before answering questions. It is obvious that the assessment objective of the two state test examples is data representation and interpretation. Further comparison of the question asked in both tests indicates that both states' test questions ask for data comparison. Mathematics is a quantitative expression in the

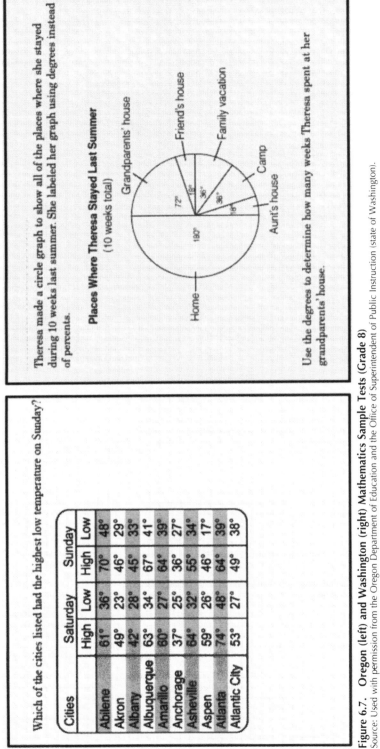

Figure 6.7. Oregon (left) and Washington (right) Mathematics Sample Tests (Grade 8)

Source: Used with permission from the Oregon Department of Education and the Office of Superintendent of Public Instruction (state of Washington).

Which of the cities listed had the highest low temperature on Sunday?

Cities	Saturday		Sunday	
	High	Low	High	Low
Abilene	61°	36°	70°	48°
Akron	49°	23°	46°	29°
Albany	42°	28°	45°	33°
Albuquerque	63°	34°	67°	41°
Amarillo	60°	27°	64°	39°
Anchorage	37°	25°	36°	27°
Asheville	64°	32°	55°	34°
Aspen	59°	26°	46°	17°
Atlanta	74°	48°	64°	39°
Atlantic City	53°	27°	49°	38°

Theresa made a circle graph to show all of the places where she stayed during 10 weeks last summer. She labeled her graph using degrees instead of percents.

Places Where Theresa Stayed Last Summer
(10 weeks total)

Grandparents' house
Friend's house
Family vacation
72°
18°
36°
36°
Camp
180°
Aunt's house
18°
Home

Use the degrees to determine how many weeks Theresa spent at her grandparents' house.

real world. One sees charts and graphs in newspaper articles and television reports. Who then can argue against the importance of data interpretation in numeracy and mathematics literacy?

As with the English language arts (reading) state test discussed earlier, one can trace data representation and interpretation back to the mathematics learning standard regardless of the state tests compared. 2(HP) teachers know all too well that a mathematics lesson not based on the state learning standards does not prepare the students for the high-stakes state examination.

To compare the state tests further, we will analyze the high school state science tests in Oregon and Washington (figure 6.8). Both test items ask the test taker to study an experiment set up before answering questions, whether the set up is in physical science (i.e., a chemistry reaction experiment) or in life science (bean plant experiment).

Sam and Jordan are studying the reaction between vinegar and baking soda. They already know that when vinegar and baking soda are mixed a vigorous reaction produces a lot of bubbles and that the baking soda seems to disappear during the reaction. During a class discussion, the students figured out that the equation for the reaction is:

Vinegar + **Baking Soda** → **Carbon Dioxide + Water + Sodium Acetate**
CH3COOH + NaHCO3 → CO2 + H2O + Na(CH3COO)

Sam and Jordan measure 50 mL of vinegar and pour it into a flask. Then they weigh out 10 g of baking soda. Sam starts the stopwatch when Jordan dumps the baking soda into the flask, then Jordan gently swirls the flask while Sam watches to see when the last bubbles are given off by the reaction. They have determined that the reaction takes 30 sec. under these conditions.

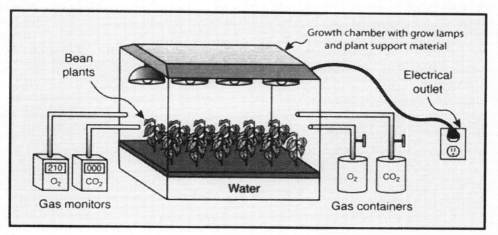

Figure 6.8.   Oregon (top) and Washington (bottom) Science Sample Tests (High School)
Source: Used with permission from the Oregon State Department of Education and the Office of Superintendent of Public Instruction (state of Washington).

In a very similar way, the objective of both state tests is scientific inquiry dealing with experimental variables that can be traced back to the state learning standard. The Oregon test asks for the change of reaction time of the experiment if the mass of baking soda changes from 10 to 5 grams. The Washington test asks whether the amount of carbon dioxide in parts per million in the chamber may change the dry mass of the bean plant in grams. Good science practices such as data analysis and interpretation are described in both the Oregon and Washington science learning standards.

College-bound students in the midwestern states are very conscientious about doing well on the college admission test known as the American College Testing (ACT) program. One unique test feature that strikes fear in many students is the science reasoning test. If a science teacher is not familiar with the ACT science reasoning testing format, his or her students will be in for a big surprise. Figure 6.9 shows an ACT science reasoning item comparing the different viewpoints of two scientists. The assessment objective behind the test is in-depth reading comprehension and comparison. Science teachers who are conscientious about preparing the students well for the ACT will teach students how to compare different viewpoints in various science investigations and issues. Even a good teacher will not prepare the students well if he or she is not *teaching to the test*, and the ACT item discussed is one good example.

Teaching to the test has been a taboo among educators. It means teaching to the standardized tests that are poorly constructed and sometimes even irrelevant. The theory continues to say that teaching to the test is narrow, and it stifles creativity. Today, a new interpretation of teaching to the test is emerging. It is called *curriculum alignment*. It means teachings that are aligned sharply to the academic standards set by the state. To some people, this still might be teaching to the test! Indeed, ignoring the alignment between what is taught in the classroom and what is tested by the state can invite undesirable consequences.

A major advantage of multiple-choice examinations as illustrated in the state tests discussion above is its efficiency. The test can ask many questions, covering a wide area in a short period of time. The ease of use and the reliability of scoring are considered a plus for the user. With the aid of an answer key, many examinations can be scored quickly and uniformly. A major drawback of the multiple-choice examination, however, is its reflection on the low cognitive levels of Bloom's Taxonomy. It does take more time and expertise to write higher-level questions to test a student's ability to apply, analyze, synthesize, and evaluate.

Short-answer, or constructive-response, tests are a supplement to many multiple-choice examinations. In the tests, students are asked to explain or supply a brief answer consisting of names, words, phrases, or symbols. Short answers are common in mathematics tests in which the student is asked to show the process or calculations used to arrive at the answer. Short-answer items are relatively easy to write for a more in-depth assessment of knowledge. On the other hand, unexpected but plausible answers may be difficult to score even with a well-constructed scoring rubric.

The success of any 2(HP) schools is judged predominantly by the academic success of students performing in the state achievement tests. The setup of the state achievement test is the multiple-choice format with supplemental student constructive response; therefore, it is apparent that 2(HP) schools deliberately prepare students to demonstrate what they know in the multiple-choice and constructive-response formats.

Directions: Read the passage, and choose the best answer ro each question. You may refer to the passage as often as necessary

---

Unmanned spacecraft taking images of Jupiter's moon Europa have found its surface to be very smooth with few meteorite craters. Europa's surface ice shows evidence of being continually resmoothed and reshaped. Cracks. dark bands, and pressure ridges (created when water or slush is squeezed up between 2 slabs of ice) are commonly seen in images of the surface. Two scientists express their views as to whether the presence of a deep ocean beneath the surface is responsible for Europa's surface features.

Scientist 1

A deep ocean of liquid water exists on Europa. Jupiter's gravitational field produces tides within Europa that can cause heating of the subsurface to a point where liquid water can exist. The numerous cracks and dark bands in the surface ice closely resemble the appearance of thawing ice covering the polar oceans on Earth. Only a substantial amount of circulating liquid water can crack and rotate such large slabs of ice. The few meteorite craters that exist are shallow and have been smoothed by liquid water that oozed up into the crater from the subsurface and then quickly froze.

Jupiter's magnetic field, sweeping past Europa. would interact with the salty, deep ocean and produce a second magnetic field around Europa. The spacecraft has found evidence of this second magnetic field.

Scientist 2

No deep, liquid water ocean exists on Europa. The heat generated by gravitational tides is quickly lost to space because of Europa's small size, as shown by its very low surface temperature ($-160°C$). Many of the features on Europa's surface resemble features created by flowing glaciers on Earth. Large amounts of liquid water are not required for the creation of these features. If a thin layer of ice below the surface is much warmer than the surface ice, it may be able to flow and cause cracking and movement of the surface ice. Few meteorite craters are observed because of Europa's very thin atmosphere: surface ice continually sublimes (changes from solid to gas) into this atmosphere, quickly eroding and removing any craters that may have formed.

Which of the following best describes how the 2 scientists explain how craters are removed from Europa's surface?

	Scientist 1	Scientist 2
A.	Sublimation	Filled in by water
B.	Filled in by water	Sublimation
C.	Worn smooth by wind	Sublimation
D.	Worn smooth by wind	Filled in by water

(2) According to the information provided. which of the following descriptions of Europa would be accepted by both scientists?

A. Europa has a larger diameter than does Jupiter.
B. Europa has a surface made of rocky material.
C. Europa has a surface temperature of 20 C.
D. Europa is completely covered by a layer of ice.

Figure 6.9. ACT Science Reasoning Test Item
Source: Used with permission from ACT. www.actstudent.org.sampletest/science/sci_01.html

6.6. FROM ASSESSMENT TO EVALUATION OF STUDENT LEARNING

Once a teacher has graded the tests, homework assignments, reports, and projects, he or she will give a value indicator to reflect the merit of the work. This in essence is what evaluation is about. For most people this is done in a letter-grade scale from A to F, with A representing outstanding work; B, above-average work; C, average work;

D, below-average work; and F, failure. There are two general approaches to evaluation. One approach involves comparisons among students; this form of evaluation is called *norm-referenced evaluation*. An alternative approach involves comparisons with preestablished criteria or standards and is called *criterion-referenced evaluation*.

Norm-referenced grading assumes that student achievement in a class will vary in a group of heterogeneous students. The heterogeneity stems from the students' prior knowledge, learning styles, aptitude, and motivation. In theoretical situations, test scores will be distributed in a range from high to low, with very few low scores and very few high scores. Such a norm-referenced grading procedure is commonly called *grading on the curve*. When a group (i.e., class) of students is graded on a curve, by nature of the score distribution, some students will be at the low end and some will be at the high end; the bulk will be between the two extremes. One way of interpreting the score distribution is that some students will fail (i.e., because they are at the low end of the score distribution) regardless of their performance.

Under a criterion-referenced test system, a student's performance is determined by a comparison with a defined criterion (or standard) of achievement. For that reason, the success or failure of the other students in the test group in meeting the criterion is not important and will not be considered. Thus in a criterion-referenced grading system, any grade distribution is possible anywhere from all As to all Fs. A common guide of criterion-referenced grading is assigning letter grades according to the percentage of correct answers. For example, a score of 90% or higher is an A, 80% to 89% is a B, 70% to 79% is a C, 60% to 69% is a D, and 59% or below is an F. The range of such a grading system may adjust according to the expectations of the course, the prior knowledge of the students, or both.

Criterion-referenced testing is becoming more popular in the education arena today. Educators have come to believe that clearly established learning standards (as in the state examinations) are best evaluated with criterion-referenced examinations. Furthermore, students can master the knowledge and skills under the right learning environment. After all, is not this the premise behind the No Child Left Behind law?

Finally, before a teacher can decide what type of test to use, he or she has to consider three questions. First, does the strategy of a particular test align with the school's educational goals and objectives? Second, does the strategy address the academic content and/or processes the state assesses? Third, does the strategy allow for the kinds of interpretations state education officials wish to make about student performance? Once the teacher has answered these three questions, the task of choosing between the norm-referenced evaluation and criterion-referenced evaluation will become clear.

6.7. EFFECTIVE ASSESSMENT SUGGESTIONS

Educational objectives become the criteria by which materials are selected, content is outlined, instructional procedures are developed, and tests and examinations are prepared.

—Ralph Tyler (1949)

One significant lesson that we learned from 2(HP) schools is that assessment is not an independent activity. Assessment is by design an integral component of teaching and learning. Assessment should be student centered, and it informs instruction. Effective 2(HP) teachers seldom have the complete freedom to teach anything they choose. Rather, their teachings are guided by the state learning standards and school goals and objectives specifying what students should know and be able to do. Hence, it is important to understand that curriculum, instruction, and now assessment are all standards driven.

The view of standards-based curriculum, instruction, and assessment is not revolutionary. Ralph Tyler, then a professor at the University of Chicago, described the logic of the standards-driven process more than 60 years ago. His use of educational objectives is similar to the learning standards that educators commonly use today. A careful analysis of Tyler's statement that "educational objectives become the criteria by which . . . tests and examinations are prepared" suggests that assessment is not something that teachers do at the end of instruction. Rather, desired outcomes need to be first identified before acceptable evidence of achieving the outcome through assessment is prepared. The wisdom revealed in the operation sequence described is the backward design of instruction (figure 6.10).

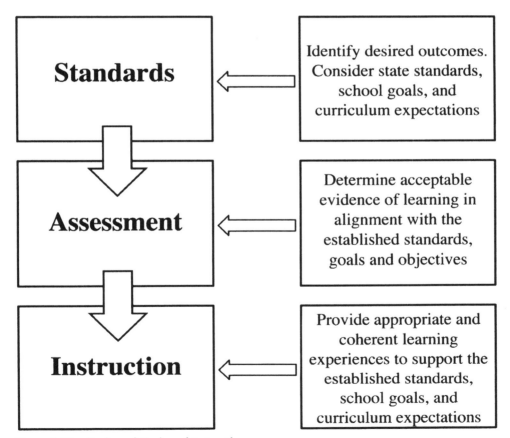

Figure 6.10.   Backward Design of Instruction
Source: Courtesy of the author.

The backward design encourages the teachers to think like the test designer before preparing a unit of instruction. It is at this stage that the teacher considers a range of assessment strategies that include a balanced use of informal and formal methods. Regardless of the methods used, the teacher needs to understand that the collection of learning evidence is not a single moment in time but an activity over time.

Let us move to more classroom suggestions now that we are done discussing the big picture of backward design in assessment.

1. Plan a course schedule of giving graded assignments and tests that will count toward a final grade. Announce the schedule well in advance so students are prepared to do well.
2. Prepare a content outline to be covered by each test. Normally, the content is classified by topics of the course.
3. Consider the purpose of each test and align that to the method of assessment. Consider both the nature of the curriculum and the characteristics of the students in choosing the method of testing. For example, decide whether a written test or a performance test is appropriate.
4. Check the level of assessment to see that different levels of cognition are measured. If the test has an overwhelming number of the what-when-where type of questions, it measures only the lowest level of the taxonomy, knowledge. How many how-why questions are in the test? They represent higher cognitive levels of the taxonomy.
5. Check the accuracy of the test items and the answer key. Are there any ambiguities? Can the teacher defend the answer when challenged?
6. Analyze the test results to improve future testing. Are there questions that no one can answer correctly? What is the implication of testing a concept that is not in the curriculum or instruction? Are there questions that all students can answer correctly? What is the purpose of testing a concept or skill that everybody knows?
7. Look at additional assessment resources on the Internet, in the media resource center, or by the office of testing and research. These resources can assist teachers to do their job more effectively in terms of writing test items, scoring, assessing individual students, and conducting score interpretation or large-group (i.e., class) test interpretation and summary.

REFERENCES

United States National Commission on Excellence in Education. 1983. *A nation at risk: The imperative for education reform: A report to the nation and the secretary of education.* Washington, DC: U.S. Department of Education.

Tyler, R. W. 1949. *Basic principles of curriculum and instruction.* Chicago: University of Chicago Press.

Wong, O., and M. L. Lam. 2007. *Using data analysis to improve student learning: Toward 100% proficiency.* Lanham, MD: Rowman & Littlefield Education.

Chapter Seven

The 2(HP) Model

Jayden is a first-year high school chemistry teacher at Saint Ethelreda School. Theresa is Jayden's mentor teacher; they share the department office. One afternoon after school, Jayden asked Theresa a pressing question about a chemistry experiment.

"*Yesterday, I could not get the experiment results right when I combined the Tylorine powder with the Tylors solution,*" said Jayden. "*What seems to be the problem?*" Theresa asked. "*The purple color after the chemical reaction came out too dark. Isn't it supposed to be just a light purple color?*" Jayden continued. "*What is your recipe for preparing the Tylorine powder? Is it a 1-to-1 mix of sodium chloride and ground phenolphthalein, or is it a 1-to-0.1 mix of sodium chloride and ground phenolphthalein?*" Theresa asked with great curiosity. "*My mixture recipe was 1 to 1,*" Jayden continued. "*There is your problem. You have too much ground phenolphthalein. Try the 1-to-0.1 recipe and the reaction color will come out light purple,*" Theresa answered quickly with a smile. Jayden replicated the Tylorine powder recipe and the experiment results came out as predicted—an instantaneous success.

Three weeks into the school year, Jayden came to Theresa with a classroom-management challenge. Jayden was not successful in ending his chemistry class in an orderly manner. Students often scrambled to finish the period and head out the door.

As a mentor teacher, Theresa invited Jayden to her class to observe and learn how her class was dismissed properly. After several observations, Jayden learned one simple rule: getting students and the room ready for the end of the class is procedural. Any equipment or materials used during instructional activities must be returned to their storage spaces. Cleanup of the work stations and the room should be completed before the end-of-the-period bell. Jayden attempted to replicate the procedural model; nevertheless, it took him several long weeks to slowly bring the students back to follow the proper dismissal procedure.

Throughout the school year, Jayden learned and replicated a number of effective science teaching models from his mentor teacher and prepared the students for the mandatory high-stakes state examination. In his teaching repertoire he implemented the strategies of tapping into students' prior knowledge and engaging students in constructivist learning with proper feedback and practices, to mention just a few. When the state test results came out, Jayden was quite disappointed to find that his students had performed only at a moderate level of success compared to his other grade-level veteran colleagues in the science department.

7.1. WHAT IS A MODEL?

A model comes in many shapes, sizes, and styles. In Jayden's scenario, he encounters and learns from three models: a chemistry reaction recipe model, a classroom-management procedural model, and several effective teaching models. The models are different in nature and in complexity. One common feature of the three models is that they all have information input and expected results output. In education, input is equated with teacher instruction and other school functions. Output, on the other hand, is often equated with student achievement and success. Based on the input and output evidences, a model matrix is developed (figure 7.1) to show the nine possible combinations of input and output.

Cell #7 represents a combination of high input and high results output. Cell #8 represents a combination of moderate input and high results output. Cell #9 represents a combination of low input and high results output. The remaining cells are self-explanatory: they show the various combinations of input and output efforts. In education, the ideal expected results of student success are always high as represented in cells #7, #8, and #9 regardless of the input levels.

Let us revisit the three models discussed earlier with Jayden. The chemistry recipe model is mathematical. The model parts are purely numerical and they are easy to follow and copy, like building a machine from parts. A replication of the model guarantees almost instantaneous success. In figure 7.1, high outputs are represented by cells #7, #8, and #9.

The second model is procedural. It involves a logarithmic behavioral set to dismiss a class properly. Due to the complexity of human variables involved, one can no longer treat this as a machine model. This model will take a bit more challenge and time to achieve success, and the output of expected results is not easy to guarantee. In figure 7.1, this can be represented by a range of outputs represented by different cell ranges, assuming that the level of information input is high.

The third model is conceptual and cultural. It involves a very complex behavioral system between the students and their environment, which includes the teacher, the school, the home, and the community. It is an extreme challenge to replicate all the pieces that are not parts of the machine. Here, the expected results of success are even harder to guarantee, assuming that the level of information input is high, moderate, or low. In figure 7.1, this is represented by an even wider range of output cells.

What can one conclude from the previous model discussion? A model is often a simplified physical and/or mental representation that people follow and use to achieve results. A machine model has standardized submodel pieces. On the other hand, a cultural model, such as education, is more difficult to standardize. The wide range of information input, or information processing, often results in various levels of results output. The replication of an education model is not like working in a factory assembly line. The education model is very complex with more-than-you-want-to-know

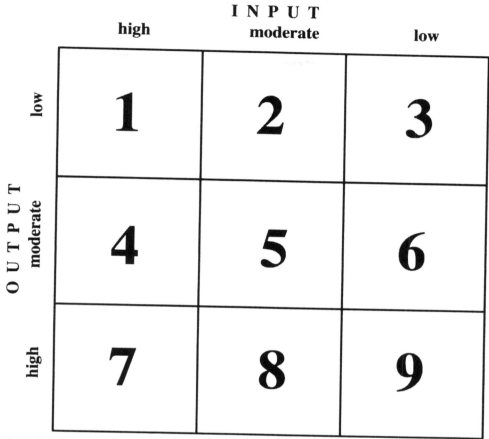

Figure 7.1. The Input-Output Model
Source: Courtesy of the author.

variables dealing with the cultivation of complex human behaviors. One can replicate the school building, the curriculum, and the textbooks of successful schools. However, one cannot replicate or clone the students, the teaching staff, and the school leaders to achieve the same expected successful results. Even more impossible to replicate are the home environment and the culture of the school community. For that reason, the replication of an education model, such as 2(HP) with expected student success, is theoretical. The good news; however, is that the 2(HP) model can still be extrapolated, allowing educators to go from the known to the unknown and achieve a certain level of student success.

7.2. WHAT ARE THE TRAITS OF THE 2(HP) MODEL?

Any site-based decision-making school councils and chief school administrators can learn from the 2(HP) model to help plan and execute school turnaround strategies.

The model can help school decision makers develop practices and policy alternatives for immediate implementation in schools. The model includes major components that lead to the practical school improvement recommendations checklist. All the practices discussed in the previous chapters should not be perceived as the only ways to improve schools. However, they should be construed as ways noted by schools as having a positive impact on student success despite the varied school implementation.

In the analysis of 2(HP) schools, particular attention was paid to the review of patterns of actions of the "beating the odds" schools with the support of evidence of positive student outcome. It is very important to note that the review of patterns definitely does not include school policy or equitable school funding, a general but important approach to school improvement. School policy and funding are the critical behind-the-scenes buttresses to sustain school improvement efforts.

In all the 2(HP) schools studied, there are distinct features. The features are having strong leadership and building a committed school staff to improve instruction, which encompasses curriculum and assessment.

Leadership

In the 2006–2007 school year, 83% of schools across the nation made the adequate yearly progress under the No Child Left Behind Act of 2001 (NCLB); 14% of schools were designated as being in need of improvement; and 3% of schools were designated as being in need of improvement and restructuring (Mapping America's Educational Progress 2008).

A failing school needs to turn around quickly, and strong leadership is key. School leaders need to make a clear commitment to change dramatically from the status quo and signal the urgency of the improvement. A number of the 2(HP) schools started the turnaround with new leaders and underwent major changes in school leadership practices. The changes are mostly rapid and substantial. The leaders demonstrated a commitment to developing a cohesive learning community focusing on the students. Specific leadership actions were framed through a child-centered lens with the belief that the school staff should have the passion, knowledge, and skills to implement strong instruction. Strong leadership often meets resistance. The turnaround leaders skillfully struck a balance between developing a collaborative culture and demanding a change.

An instructional leadership role is pivotal to turning low-performing schools around. Typical leadership that signals change in a low-performing school is the establishment of a stronger direction for the school in teaching and learning. The leader spends more time in the classrooms monitoring both teacher and student performance. He or she is more accessible to staff and students, supporting an environment conducive to great learning.

The instructional leader analyzes different types of data, dealing with student achievement, discipline, class size, use of instructional time, and staffing. He or she brings the staff into the process to identify what is and is not working. Eventually, the leader eliminates practices that do not work and replaces them with strategies that work.

An instructional leader shares leadership and practices consensus decision making. He or she learns more openly among stakeholders with an increased value of mutual support to ensure the well-being of both students and staff. Many 2(HP) school principals share leadership by working with a leadership team or lead teachers. This way, the voice of the staff in school decisions is strengthened in assuming mutual responsibilities for student results.

There are potential roadblocks to school improvement. The school community may believe that the school will not change or does not have the potential to change. Some believe that improvement efforts come and go, and they just wait for the improvement simply to go with no commitment of efforts. Reform leaders need to show the spectators some quick changes to dispel the entrenched mind-sets that the school will never change. Some quick school changes may include holding meetings with the community and inviting parents to visit classes.

A shared common attitude that all students can learn is essential to any successful school. Thus, building a committed staff comprised of people with the same mind-set is essential. A cohesive staff setting high expectations for student success is seen commonly across 2(HP) schools. A committed staff cares about students, the school, and themselves. They are diligent and doing whatever it takes to meet the goal of raising student achievement. Many 2(HP) school leaders take the time to meticulously choose and deploy the right staff members for the school. By the same token, the 2(HP) school leaders also take action to remove staff members who are incompetent or resistant to improving the school. To have the right staff in the right places requires that the principal know the staff well. That involves spending quality time in their workplaces, such as the classrooms.

Teaching and Learning

2(HP) schools focus on improving teaching and learning at every step of the improvement process. In essence, the schools set common improvement goals, look at data to plan, and monitor the progress of the improvement efforts. Analysis of data occurs on three levels: the school (NCLB requirements), the classroom (teacher effectiveness), and the student (learning needs and achievement).

Many 2(HP) schools use school-performance data to determine areas of teaching and learning that needed improvement. From the review of data, the schools develop school improvement plans and make decisions about needed changes. All 2(HP) schools make changes to directly improve instruction. Some common approaches are teacher collaboration (horizontally among sections of the same grade level, and vertically across different grade levels), use of more technology-assisted instruction, and allotment of more time for instructional planning that is aligned to the state learning standards.

Professional development focusing on instructional goals to improve student achievement is common. Staff members are engaged in an array of professional development opportunities targeted at improving critical knowledge (i.e., content and pedagogy) areas and skills (i.e., class management and time management). To be effective, professional development is often job embedded.

Schools align the curriculum and align that to the state learning standards. A meticulous curriculum review helps to ensure that teachers are teaching the knowledge and skills that students need to succeed on assessments, especially the high-stakes state assessments, the college entrance examinations, and other benchmark assessments.

7.3. SCHOOL SELF-ASSESSMENT AGAINST THE 2(HP) TRAITS

The evidence of 2(HP) school successes is quite plentiful. One may think of using the evidence as a guide to drive the next generation of successful schools regardless of their social economic status. Like other guides, the 2(HP) guide below has a checklist of specific recommendations. To be effective, the recommendation items are not to be taken in isolation to tackle a multifaceted challenge. The understanding is that each item is connected to a specific level of nonstatistical, or qualitative, evidence connecting to what worked in the 2(HP) schools. More important, the guide may vary according to the time investment as well as the expertise and the experience of the users. The consolidated categories of leadership, teaching, and instruction are selected according to the study analysis of the 2(HP) schools. Regardless of its social economic status, any school may self-assess against the checklist below to better understand its status of success and efforts toward improvement. If the school scores 48 or better (out of a total of 60 points), it has a good chance of being successful. If the self-assessment scores 57 or better, the school is on its way going from good to excellent!

(1) LEADERSHIP
In the following checklist, 1 = do not know, 2 = no evidence, 3 = little evidence,
      4 = strong evidence

1a The leader communicates a clear purpose to school staff.	1 2 3 4
1b The leader creates high expectations for success.	1 2 3 4
1c The leader shares authority and decision making.	1 2 3 4
1d The leader prioritizes areas of improvement.	1 2 3 4
1d The leader shows a willingness to make the same changes asked of the staff.	1 2 3 4
1e The leader is an instructional leader visible in classrooms.	1 2 3 4
1f The leader assesses the strengths and weaknesses of the staff.	1 2 3 4
1g The leader deploys staff members with valuable skills.	1 2 3 4
1h The leader replaces staff members who resists the school's improvement efforts.	1 2 3 4
1i The leader recruits new staff with needed specialized skills	1 2 3 4

(2) TEACHING and LEARNING

2a Curriculum aligns with state and local standards.	1 2 3 4
2b Curriculum meets the learning needs of all students.	1 2 3 4
2c School staff involved in the collaborative development of curriculum.	1 2 3 4
2d Analyze student achievement data to identify gaps in student learning.	1 2 3 4
2e Analyze student formative data to drive and improve instruction.	1 2 3 4
2f Prioritize areas of instructional focus to improve student learning.	1 2 3 4
2g Monitor student progress and readjust strategies of improvement.	1 2 3 4
2h Arrange for targeted professional development to support instruction.	1 2 3 4

7.4. 2(HP) SCHOOLS LEADING THE
WAY TO A WORLD-CLASS EDUCATION

We need the best and the brightest in our profession. And I guarantee, at the end of the day, you will feel like you made a difference. Of course, I'm a little biased. I'm a teacher.

—Eric Langhorst,
2008 Missouri Teacher of the Year
(Kauchak and Eggen 2011)

To achieve the status of world-class education means shared responsibility among teachers, school leaders, parents, and other school community stakeholders.

From the moment students walk into a school, the most important success factor is the teacher standing in the front of the classroom. It is not the income of their family, nor the color of their skin. To ensure the success of the students, schools have to do a better job recruiting, developing, supporting, retaining, and rewarding effective teachers. Teachers should be recognized on the basis of student growth and learning. Without looking around too hard, one can observe that 2(HP) school teachers are competent, committed, and supported. They are given the time to prepare, collaborate, and lead, and the respect that all professionals deserve. A good teacher can motivate and help students to achieve. On the other hand, a bad teacher allows students to slip through the cracks and fail.

School leaders, especially the principals, are responsible for creating an orderly environment for work. They are open to fundamental changes to set high standards for teaching and learning. They identify needs based on achievement results with broad input from the entire school community, and they monitor the progress. Principals are active learners themselves; they learn from other successful schools and seek continuous professional development for themselves as well as the school staff.

2(HP) parents and other concerned people in the school community often make their voices heard. They work closely with the school to make it the best learning environment for children. Parents instill order and discipline at home to reinforce school rules; some even volunteer to monitor school halls and playgrounds. Through the diligent work of the parent-teacher association, parents support the school improvement efforts and let the school staff know that they are heading in the right direction.

2(HP) schools pave the road to a world-class education. They foster the effectiveness of classroom teachers and school leaders, and they develop collaboration between the school and the school community.

Race to the Top

In 2009, President Barack Obama and Secretary of Education Arne Duncan announced a $4.35 billion U.S. Department of Education program to jump-start reforms in public education (U.S. Department of Education 2010). The program is funded by the ED Recovery Act as part of the 2009 American Recovery and Reinvestment Act.

State application for Race to the Top funding is evaluated on a selection of criteria worth a total of 500 points. Many people may not understand the intricacy of the selection criteria; however, it is worth noting that the top weight of the criteria is "great teachers and leaders." The subcriteria under "great teachers and leaders" are:

- Improve teacher and principal effectiveness based on performance
- Ensure equitable distribution of effective teachers and principals
- Provide high-quality pathways for aspiring teachers and principals
- Provide effective support to teachers and principals
- Improve the effectiveness of teacher and principal preparation programs

It is also important to note that the inclusion of turning around and intervening in low-performing schools is a part of the Race to the Top selection criteria. States with 2(HP) schools already have a school-reform prototype helping them to be competitive in the Race to the Top application.

REFERENCES

Kauchak, D., and P. Eggen. 2011 *Introduction to teaching: Becoming a professional*. 4th ed. Pearson Education.

Mapping America's Educational Process. 2008. www.2ed.gov/nclb/accountability/results/progress/nation.html.

U.S. Department of Education. 2009. *Race to the Top Program executive summary*. At www.2ed.gov/programs/racetothetop/executive-summary.pdf (accessed January 26, 2010).

U.S. Department of Education. 2010. *A blueprint for reform: The reauthorization of the Elementary and Secondary Education Act*. Washington, DC: U.S. Department of Education.

Conclusion

Through many years, American education has gone down a long and winding road to attain the desirable outcomes of producing successful students. In 1983, the quality of American education was described in *A Nation at Risk*. The report pointed out the problems that infested the American education system. In 1994, the Goals 2000: Educate America Act was established. The act set goals to improve student achievement. In 2001, No Child Left Behind (NCLB) became law, so students and schools are held to new levels of accountability. Under NCLB, by 2014 all students are to meet and exceed the proficiency standards for reading and mathematics.

President Barack Obama admitted that NCLB is flawed, and a new, reenvisioned federal role in education is proposed to strengthen America's public education system with reference to college and career preparation through working with stakeholders at all levels. In the words of President Obama,

> Every child in America deserves a world-class education. Today, more than ever, a world-class education is a prerequisite for success. America was once the best-educated nation in the world. A generation ago, we led all nations in college completion, but today, 10 countries have passed us. It is not that their students are smarter than ours. It is that these countries are being smarter about how to educate their students. And the countries that out-educate us today will out-compete us tomorrow. We must do better. Together, we must achieve a new goal, that by 2020, the United States will once again lead the world in college completion. We must raise the expectations for our students, for our schools, and for ourselves—this must be a national priority. We must ensure that every student graduates from high school well prepared for college and a career. A world-class education is also a moral imperative—the key to securing a more equal, fair, and just society. We will not remain true to our highest ideals unless we do a far better job of educating each one of our sons and daughters. We will not be able to keep the American promise of equal opportunity if we fail to provide a world-class education to every child. (U.S. Department of Education 2010)

2(HP) schools uniquely represent excellence in our nation's public education system. An understanding of how they work is requisite to helping schools to improve and excel. 2(HP) schools are not machines; they represent a culture of high expectations and unquestionable commitment to excellence in education. In time, only when the 2(HP) culture is nurtured and diffused, it is hopeful that the United States will once again lead the world in education.

REFERENCES

U.S. Department of Education. 2008. Mapping America's educational progress. At www .ed.gov/nclb/accountability/results/progress/nation.html (accessed February 29, 2008).

U.S. Department of Education. 2010. *A blueprint for reform: The reauthorization of the Elementary and Secondary Education Act*. Washington, DC: U.S. Department of Education.

About the Author

Ovid K. Wong is currently an associate professor of education at Benedictine University in Lisle, Illinois. He received his BSc from the University of Alberta, his MEd from the University of Washington, and his PhD in curriculum and instruction from the University of Illinois. His experience in public education spans over 20 years from the Chicago inner-city classroom to the suburban office of the assistant school superintendent. In 1989, Dr. Wong received the National Science Foundation's Outstanding Science Teacher in Illinois Award and the National Science Teaching Achievement Recognition (STAR) Award by the National Science Teachers Association. In the same year he was invited to the former Soviet Union as the environmental science delegation leader with the student ambassador program. In 1992, he was the first recipient of the Outstanding Alumni Award by the University of Alberta, and in 1995 he was the first recipient of the Distinguished Alumni Award by the College of Education at the University of Illinois. He is the author of 26 books and has received the Midwest Book Author Award from the Children's Reading Roundtable of Chicago. His 12 recent books are dedicated to coaching teachers and students to effectively prepare for the state-mandated examinations across the nation, with specific editions for Illinois, Michigan, New York, and Ohio. Dr. Wong is married with two adult children.